To Patsy

Irish Stew

by Rose Gotsis

Love,
Terry

Contents

	Page
The Blight on Avon Place	1
Patrick the Patriarch	7
The Young Storyteller	20
Nickel Day at Revere Beach	28
Pies and Parents	34
Hail Mary	40
My Influential Aunt	45
Fashionable Frannie	55
Just Another Sunday	65
He Came in a Cup	75
The Kitchen Table	83
I Hardly Knew John	89
The News About Arthur	100
Marguerite's Heart	110
Frank's Way	120
Requiem for Harry	132
The Pretty Sister	142
Last One to Wed	157
Maggie and Jack	167
The Family Secret	176

Cover design by Eleanor Randall.
Book layout by Pat Dacey.

For additional copies of this book contact:

Cassue Publications
38 Carlton Drive
Holliston, MA 01746

ISBN: 0-9744435-0-6

Gratitude for:

My parents, Maggie and Jack, my brothers, sisters, and the other relatives who filled my life with enough love and aggravation to make my life interesting.

My children, grandchildren and great grandchild, who put up with my eccentricities and my biggest fan, my husband George A. Gotsis, Sr.

My writer friends, all the members of my writer's groups who, as I read my family stories aloud, not only critiqued them, but laughed and cried when I hoped they would.

My teachers and the conferences I have attended.

Cape Cod Writers Conference

New England Writers of Vermont

Sunkist Writers of St. Petersburg, Florida

The following people who have made a special effort to encourage me to publish this book.

Dee Basch, Sandi Bernstein and Rhoda Kaplan, Louise Gandolfi, Ruth Harriet Jacobs, Terry Malcolm, Joan Millman, the late Sister Margaret Potts, RCE, Eleanor Randall, and Dawn Lesley Stewart.

– Rose Gotsis

Irish Stew

Irish-American Memoirs and Essays

By Rose Gotsis

Irish Stew is made from mutton: the meat of an old sheep. Mutton must simmer for hours to render it chewable. As a child, I not only hated the taste, I hated the smell of it cooking, but since my mother was born in Ireland and my father in South Boston, it was weekly fare. A large family has little time for finicky eaters and so I removed carrots, potatoes and turnips from the pot, washed them in hot water and mashed them with butter or I ate bread and molasses.

When I lifted the lid on my past, my family stories beckoned to be told. They came to me one at a time over a period of years, not in chronological order. So, between these pages some incidents, like my family members, appear more than once. I selected stories I liked best, and tried to make them palatable to my reader. You will see my parents did not raise orchids, they raised wildflowers. We each were allowed to grow in our own direction. There was a lot of humor, faith, and courage and a dash of acid. Recollecting often hurt, but I found gifts I never knew I possessed.

My parents raised eight children, a ninth died as an infant. I am their only surviving child. I believe those who have left this earth for another consciousness remain with us always. Whether we loved, hated or feared them, if they mattered at all, we can, if we choose, uncover their imprints on our lives. Children in a large family seldom get enough attention, so I have felt obliged to have my siblings heard.

The reader might like to know, the smell of lamb cooking sickened me until I met and married a first-generation Greek. Greeks eat a lot of lamb. When I refused to cook or eat it, my husband cooked it for me. He baked it with garlic, thyme, rosemary, vine-ripened tomatoes and olive oil, and so he changed forever my relationship with lamb. Experience changes who we are, how we act, but memory, though it deceives us for own protection, molds our minds and shapes our lives.

My values came from this so-called dysfunctional family, and like many children raised during the depression by uneducated but wise, immigrant parents, I have managed to function well. I hasten to add — my recipes come from elsewhere — I make my stew with beef.

The Blight on Avon Place

When I saw Shirley Temple in Heidi, I thought how much her loving grandfather looked like my grandfather. The resemblance ended there. Ebenezer Scrooge had a better disposition than Grandpa Nolan.

Because our house on Avon Place stood three stories high with four bedrooms, the word was out in Cork and Sligo: when you get off the boat in Boston, make your first stop Margaret and Jack's. My parents provided room and board to Irish immigrant cousins without charge, so how could they refuse to take in my mother's father who lived nearby in Cambridge and could no longer care for himself.

Though they had eight children, and had just lost an infant son, they were blessing-counters endowed with a Catholic stewardship to help the needy. Their blessing counting often made their own children miserable. Required to sleep on attic cots, or the living room sofa to support our parent's generosity, we were supposed to smile at the prospects of any new boarder.

Despite the tiny closets and single bath, the boarders posed no real problem. Once they got a toehold in the American dream, they moved out. But the "ole man", as Grandpa Nolan's children called him behind his back, was a freebie and a constant. If calling your father the "ole man" seems disrespectful, it was intended. No one liked Grandpa. He disturbed our household at a time when my father's steady employment made our lives full and pleasant.

We took Grandpa in when my mother's oldest bachelor brother left Boston for a better job in Chicago. She took Grandpa because her six siblings would not. The words "He's my father" covered his room and board, and a monthly stipend from the brother in Chicago bought the ole man's tobacco and medication. What he earned from shoemaking, he clasped to his hairy, white chest in a small black purse he strung around his short thick neck.

A farmer and shoemaker in Ireland, he came to the States in 1885 with his wife and seven children to seek his fortune making shoes for wealthy Bostonians he called "high muckamucks". Grandpa made decent money, but characteristically, he drank most of it. Alcoholism was an accepted curse in Irish culture, so it was forgivable, but Grandpa beat his saintly wife and their children. That he beat them was considered his right. That he beat their mother was behavior his children never forgave. "God rest his soul" was not the sentiment expressed when my deceased Grandfather's name was mentioned. For him, Hell was a given.

My good-natured father had built Grandpa a long cobbler's bench that ran along the large bedroom wall below the two windows that overlooked the kitchen court yard below. On the second floor, it was the best of the four bedrooms in the three-story house. Warm rays of the mid-morning sun backlighted his stunning shock of white, coarse hair as he sat bent over his bench. From the back, Grandpa looked like jovial Santa. In a one-piece union suit, no shirt, stained blue-serge pants and red suspenders, he held tiny tacks in his mouth and tapped skillfully and incessantly. The pungent smell of leather, chemicals, offensive body odor, edged with the aroma of Edgeworth's Cut Plug tobacco overwhelmed anyone who entered his room.

Mornings our kitchen was frantic. My mother had the boarders to feed before they went off to work, and children to ready for school. Patrick, the youngest, and I would play in a corner until everyone left.

"Please Rosie, do Mum a favor and bring Grandpa his morning tea," my mother asked. "He's been yelling for it all morning."

"Do I have to?" I whined.

"Yes, you do." My father patted my head affectionately. "Be a big girl. Help your mother." Young as I was, I knew, I was being used. A morning confrontation with Grandpa could ruin my mother's disposition for the day.

My small feet climbed the stairs slowly, eyes fixed on the big ironstone cup, as if my watching would prevent a spill. My hands trembled, but by the grace of God, nary a drop spilled.

"Empty my trash while yer here," he said gruffly when I placed the tea on the bench. Without looking at me, he gestured toward his wastebasket.

I picked up the tin cylinder, big as myself, watching as he poured tea into the saucer. He blew on it. Then placed his lips on the saucer's edge, and slurped loud enough to be heard in the attic bedrooms. He rose from his stool, slowly, headed toward me with cup and saucer in hand. I felt he might cuff me on the ear, as he always threatened if we made noise on the landing outside his bedroom. Felt slippers shuffled by me to the hallway.

"Is it piss or tea you're giving me Margaret?" he shouted at the top of the stairs to the top of his lungs to my mother in the kitchen below. He turned to me with tea in hand, snarled as if I were a party to the offense.

"Take this swill gurl and throw it down the toilet." I dropped the basket to take the tea. Trash spilled onto the floor. My small heart beat as he boomed, "And bring yer grandfather a daysant cup." Huge hands wiped his unshaven chin. "Then come back and clean up the unholy mess you made."

I dissolved in sobs my mother heard downstairs. She was soon at his bedroom door.

"Don't mind your Grandpa, Luv, he's not well." She took the cup and saucer from my hand. "Go downstairs like a good girl." She stood aproned and tall, then closed the door after me. Feeling a failure, I remained in the hall to listen.

"Are you daft, Pa," she shouted, "the child is not yet six. And I'll tell you once more, you'll not treat my children as you treated me or you'll be sent to the poor farm where the rest of your children believe you belong."

"When you were her age, you were picking potatoes in the field."

"How can I forget?" Now they were both shouting.

I scurried down the stairs, but not before I heard him yell.

"I'm warning you, Margaret, they'll melt in the rain." I heard my mother storm out and slam the door.

"Well at least she's not afraid of a bathtub, like you." She was halfway down the stairs when she shouted this.

Agitation showed on her face as she made him a stronger cup of tea, a bowl of oatmeal and two slices of buttered toast. All of which trembled when she picked up the tray to deliver it herself.

His tantrums had the power to terrify until the hearse took him to his grave five years later. Grandpa and the player piano moved with us to a new, larger house in the country. My brothers and I avoided him as we would a strict priest in confession. What lurked in the soul of this angry old man was seldom discussed. Little time was spent examining or excusing behavior in those days. Today, they'd probably put

Grandpa on Prozac and he'd be fine. His only good deed was to bring his children to America for a better life. In spite of his example, they were all hard working men and women who used faith rather than alcohol to handle stress.

When his embalmed body was stretched out in our parlor in 1935, I was ten years old. I was glad he was dead and refused to say a prayer at the kneeler.

"You're obliged to pay your respects to your dead grandfather," my mother said "The commandment obliges us to honor our parents, even if we don't feel affection for them."

Then an older brother, Frank, whispered something in my ear that helped me change my mind and gave me the opportunity to please my mother. He suggested I say what he had said.

I knelt on the velvet kneeler, looked into Grandpa's rouged and pasty face. Rosary beads in his cobbler's chewed-up hands rested on his chest. He looked presentable and peaceful, but he didn't fool me for a minute.

I blessed myself piously and said, "Go straight to hell, you old Fart." Only Frank had the courage to use the "B" word.

In an antique store, recently, a blue, empty tin of Edgeworth Cut tobacco took me back to Grandpa in the house on Avon place. In that instant, I knew why the smell of new leather always nauseates me.

Patrick the Patriarch

When I grew up, the Irish parents I knew considered a priest in the family God's assurance that they were good parents. What I never understood is why they never held in equal esteem the bachelor or spinster who stayed at home to care for them as they aged. Surely, God must have ordained such a vocation, as it demanded an abundance of patience, charity and sacrifice. In my mother's family of four girls and three boys, Patrick, the eldest, somehow got this difficult job, and child that I was, I knew my Grandfather took his care-taking son for granted. Not I. Whenever Uncle Pat appeared at the front door of our Avon Place house, I shouted with giddy excitement.

"He's here, Uncle Pat's here." His strong hands, large as saucepans, would scoop my four-year-old body off the foyer floor to give me an airplane ride above his head.

"Loop-da-loop," he'd shout, as I swished back and forth through air. Then he would set me down on the scatter rug as if I were made of Irish Beleek. By then Patrick, the youngest, would be standing right behind me waiting his turn.

"Do me again," I would beg after he put his name-sake down.

"God love yer. Yer old Uncle is out of breath." His deep, silver voice pealed throughout the rooms of our three-story house. He kissed my cheek, and said, "Now where's ya Mum?"

For years after my grandmother died, my mother's oldest brother and her father came to dinner every other Sunday. On alternate Sundays, they would dine with other siblings who lived in proximity to our family. When the house reeked of cabbage, I knew Pat and Grandpa Nolan would soon arrive. Spare ribs or smoked shoulder, my grandfather's favorite meal, was never cooked without it. Before they left, Uncle Pat would press pennies into our tiny palms.

"They'll expect it every time now, you big omidon," Grandpa Nolan scolded. He was right about the former but not the latter. Pat was no omidon. A bright, articulate man, his wisdom loomed over his siblings' lives with silent authority. With military posture and broad shoulders, this six-foot-three man impressed anyone he encountered.

Limited to a fifth grade education in Ireland, with his good looks and proclivity for leadership, he should have gone to college and beyond. A voracious reader, he had a gift for language. He dispensed judicious advice on everything from mortgages to marriage. His siblings listened because with advice, he often loaned, or sometimes gave them money they needed.

"Not to eejits," he said to a nephew. "You'll get nary a farthing from me to spend on drink."

Then one Sunday after dinner, his huge hands nervously raking the mass of curly black hair, he asked if he could speak to my parents alone. He plunked Grandpa in a chair in the small, dirt backyard of our urban Boston row house.

"Sing for Grandpa, kiddos. Entertain him." Fat chance. Grandpa told us to shut up and to leave the door to the dining room ajar so he could hear.

Pat told my parents he had a chance to work as a supervisor for a newspaper press in Chicago.

"There's lots in it for me, Maggie. If you take care of Pa til I find a flat."

After they left, my father paced the kitchen linoleum as my mother stared into her tea.

"For the love of God, Maggie, how can you take in the father you hate? You've enough to do with the boarders, the children."

"It's not forever. Pat deserves a vacation from his nibs. Jack, please, sit down, you're making me nervous." He sat; she took both his hands. "Listen to me. Pat cared for Mum when she was sick, and he's been stuck with Pa since she died. When we were kiddos 'twas he who stood up to a drunken Pa. He intercepted many a blow meant for my Mum or us kids. I owe him."

"What about your sisters or brothers?"

"They told Pat to send him to the poor farm. I can't do that. He's my father."

"I suppose,"my father said, his hand stroking his chin as if he might find another solution. "They'd slip the old crank a black pill."

That's how Grandpa Nolan came to live with us. Every time Pat arranged for Grandpa to move to Chicago with him, Grandpa feigned illness and called for the priest to administer last rites. Temporary became long term; now, every month Pat sent fifteen dollars.

Distance made my Uncle's homecomings more exciting. My mother rounded up the clan."Pat's coming. Pat's coming," she'd shout into the telephone.

Between visits I recognized his scrawling handwriting before I mastered reading.

"It's a letter from Uncle Pat," I'd shout after picking his letter from the thin lipped mail slot. I'd dash to the kitchen knowing my delivery would elicit a smile from my mother. As if Gospels, she read Pat's letters to all of us at the supper table. Flourishing letters about Roosevelt, the National Recovery Act and Father Couglin, and a check to cover Grandpa's care. He wrote like a reporter for the Chicago Tribune instead of the typesetter he was.

When we moved from citified Avon Place to the country, Grandpa and the upright player piano moved with us. Uncle Pat came to visit him by train from

Chicago every six weeks. By now, Uncle Pat's name was scratched from my nightly-prayer list. He lost his pedestal after I took my first turn emptying Grandpa's chamber pot. We kids retched at the odor of the old man's urine while he acted as if emptying his piss was a granted privilege.

Despite my holy castigation of Uncle Pat, in 1935, the same year Grandpa died, Pat became president of his union.

"I'm not surprised," my mother said, when she read his letter. "He ran for Alderman in Cambridge once and won, but when his parish record arrived from Ireland it said he was too young. Pat minded losing the job alright, but minded more the folks didn't even know his birth date."

The same year Pat was promoted and Grandpa Nolan died, my father lost his job as Traffic Manager with the Sand and Gravel Company. The bank foreclosed on our house, and we moved back to the less expensive city. Uncle Pat sent Grandpa's allowance post mortem knowing my folks needed help. His visits were less frequent, his letters fewer, but his check came every month. In one letter that contained a check we got big news. Uncle Pat was getting married.

"Gertie, my bride-to-be, has herself a fine job," Pat wrote when he was fifty. "She's forty, a supervisor with the Telephone Company." Excited to extravagance, my mother actually telephoned long distance to congratulate him.

"Sure and there's no need of you coming to Chicago. They'll be no rolling back of the rugs and step dancing for this wedding. We're too old for nonsense. Use yer money for important things,"he said. My mother, Aunt Nora, and Uncle John went anyhow. When they returned details were scarce.

"Gertie is a friendly plain type you'd expect a wise man like Uncle Pat to marry. Pat says she's loaded with dough," my mother said, when I asked about Pat's bride. Though we thought we now had two wealthy relatives, Pat's letters now came without checks. Work was scarce for my father. We missed Pat's money, but, fortunately, two older siblings found work. When World War II got underway, my family's financial status improved.

By 1942, my father worked steady. Two brothers sent home army allotments. Even my mother loved her job putting tarter sauce on the scrod plates behind the counter of Thompson's Spa in downtown Boston. After high school, I got a clerk's job in the Telephone Company.

When my brother Harry finished his missions overseas in the Air Corps, he came home and married a girl he had met in California. My mother could now afford to travel to his West Coast wedding by Pullman. On her way home, she visited Uncle Pat and Gertie in Chicago. Details of my brother's elaborate wedding were overshadowed by Pat's sad plight.

"Gertie is a skinflint," my mother ranted, unpacking her suitcase like a runaway child angrily packs to leave home. "She wears cheap, gun-metal lisle stockings and she's too cheap to fix her broken bridgework. Lights and radio go off at 8:00 p.m. She buys day old bread at the A & P and skimps on food. She has a fine pension from the Telephone Company, but she works as a switchboard operator at a downtown hotel. Pat ignores her stinginess. I told him what I thought of her. If he wants to see me again, he'll have to come to Boston."

He did. After that, every summer we drove to the Greyhound bus station to pick up an agile Uncle Pat. "God Luv yer for coming," he'd shout running across the terminal when he spied us. He toted one of the battered leather suitcases the Nolans had carried from Ireland years before.

"Tis grand to visit you fine folks. Gertie works all day so I'm alone." Thick bushy graying eyebrows slashed across his now watery blue eyes. He looked like a cross between two of his heroes, James Michael Curley, ex-mayor of Boston, and John L. Lewis, head of the miners' union. In our two-family house on a busy street in Everett, Massachusetts he sat by the bay window as if he had a view of Cape Cod Bay. When his siblings and my cousins visited, Pat sat in our big, maroon-velvet overstuffed living room chair and dispensed advice.

"Don't be giving F. W. Woolworth's a penny," he scolded, when a cousin said where he bought his son's toy truck. "The damn trinkets Americans buy there come from Japan. Who do you think put the bastards on their feet so they could bomb Pearl Harbor?"

"A good civil service job. Steady and secure. That's what you should go after," he advised me when I said I wanted a job in publishing or advertising.

He'd argue the merits of organized labor, the oppressive methods of big business, impressing upon us the hardships of pre-union days. My brothers and I opposed him merely for the sake of argument. We knew he'd have voted for a Basset hound if it ran on the Democratic ticket.

He loved to visit Suffolk Downs, Revere Beach, Harvard Square, and downtown Boston. My brother Pat drove him to visit old cronies on Huron Ave. in Cambridge. My brother said Uncle Pat passed out what he called a finner or a sawbuck to people down on their luck. We rejected money Uncle Pat offered, and though he had become as frugal as his wife, he seemed disappointed that we were no longer needy. Young Patrick and I invited him to a movie one night and his refusal prompted a dissertation.

"Spend your hard earned money on movies if you want but not for me. Hollywood is robbery. I paid to see Al Jolson in *Sonny Boy*. For the luv of God, a grown man crying. T'was nothing but drivel." As far as I know, he never paid to see another movie.

Sallow and thin, the summer before he died, he visited us. We knew something was wrong when he no longer relished the blood pudding my father fried for his breakfast or my mother's mutton stew. My mother urged him to see her doctor. Pat refused. He insisted he was fine.

"Gertie is so cheap, she probably shrunk his stomach," my mother whispered to me.

I see him now as he sat by the window watching traffic on Ferry Street all day. In wide, red suspenders over a sleeveless undershirt, navy blue, penciled-striped pants, and black kidskin shoes. All his clothes now appeared too large.

"What's up, Uncle Pat?" I said one day when I came home from work. His face so pensive, I concluded he was pondering the Taft-Hartley Law or Harry Truman's ability to preside, or I expected a discourse on what he read in the morning Globe.

"Be good while you're young, Rosie, me luv," he held up black rosary beads pinched in his fingers. "You see before you an old man, squeezing the beads and sucking around God in his old age trying to get on his good side." You still needed a sharp scythe to cut his Irish brogue and his voice was solemn.

"C'mon, Uncle Pat. You're a good man," I said, filled with a sudden sadness at the possibility of losing him.

He held his belly and laughed, deep and resonant.

"So 'tis a saint you think your old Uncle is? You say, I don't need God's forgiveness. That's a good one," he said, slapping his knee.

"Grandpa should have groveled for God's forgiveness. Not you. My Mum thinks you're a saint."

"'Twas fear that drove poor Pa, Rosie. Ireland was grim, and this country wasn't much better for him. Imagine bringing seven kids here and them not yet sixteen." Holding his belly again, he now grimaced in pain. Something was eating him. "'Twas hard on the ole man learning new ways."

We lost Pat to stomach cancer before the next summer. Gertie didn't tell us until he was interred. She quoted his last wishes. "No fanfare, the last rights and a Requiem High Mass. Give everyone who did for me my love and thanks."

By now, my cousin Joe had discovered Gertie was, heaven forbid, a Protestant. No wonder Uncle Pat didn't want the family at his wedding. And it was typical of our Irish-Catholic parents not to mention this to their children. We determined that was why there was no talk of the wedding when they all returned from Chicago. Their flawless brother had risked his immortal soul by marrying Gertie in a Protestant ceremony.

Pat's money went to the now, not-so-beloved wife Gertie. He told me his wife was a money-pinching crab, but he had told my mother Gertie was a "grand ole girl".

My mother kept in touch with Gertie after Uncle Pat died. When I acted surprised, she said, "It's simply because Gertie honored Pat's request for the last rites and a Requiem Mass when he died."

Years later, Gertie visited Boston shortly after my father died. By now we were all married. Time heals even Irish grudges, so my mother looked forward to her visit. I think she expected the two widows would melt in consolation.

"I can't stand the woman," she confessed a week later. She telephoned me in Maine where I then lived. She had to talk fast, Gertie was still asleep. "She hasn't spent a dime of the quarter-million she says Pat left. I've paid every subway fare, bought every lunch, paid for every movie ticket." My mother was exasperated. "She picked up old magazines on the train coming here, and gave them to me as if they were a house gift."

"How awful." I responded minimally, knowing she needed to vent.

"The only thing she pays for," my mother continued lowering her voice, "is her medication for epilepsy. What bothers me most is that I'm becoming stingy as she is and I hate myself. We went to Dini's Seafood for lunch and, deliberately, I went to the ladies room as the check was delivered. I kept peeking out to see if she had paid. When people started looking at me suspiciously, I went back to the table and picked up the check. I pretended I didn't have enough and asked her to leave the tip."

"Did she balk?"

"She claimed the service was shabby." When I insisted it was excellent, she fumbled forever in her bag for money. 'Don't hurry,' I said, 'I've got time to wait.' She knew I meant business. I hate being her Patsy." My mother was livid.

I gave my mother advice she always gave me. "Pray. Maybe she'll leave early." It worked. Of a three-week visit, Gertie had stayed twenty-days beyond her welcome. She left one day early to get a cut-rate fare.

In 1960, Gertie wrote from Florida, "I have moved. No more Chicago winters for me."

Two years later, we received a photograph of Gertie and her new, blonde, obviously much younger, husband. He was a neighbor in her mobile home park.

"If that omidon thinks he's getting any of her money, he's mistaken." My mother laughed, looking at the picture. Omidon, means "big fool" in Irish-speak.

About three or four years later, Gertie's only niece telephoned to say Gertie's new husband had called and said she had died in an epileptic seizure.

"It seems she forgot to take her medicine," the niece said.

"Not on your life," my mother said, "Gertie never forgot her pills."

"You mean, you suspect foul play?"

"It's a possibility." My mother seldom minced words. "She left no will. And one thing for sure, Gertie wasn't going to die unless her money went with her. Money was her first love. Never shared it with anyone while she was alive. And another thing, Gertie took her pills religiously."

It seemed no one cared enough about Gertie or the money, to investigate the circumstances surrounding her death. I pictured her former husband lolling around a pool, drinking gin and tonic with women in bikinis; spending money Gertie saved eating stale bread with her broken bridgework.

"Maybe we're wrong," my mother said when I visited her a few weeks after we received the news of Gertie's death. "Maybe the second husband is a decent chap who will put their crummy money to better use than Pat and Gertie ever did. It never seemed to give them much enjoyment. If he doesn't, and if he did what I think he did, you can rest assured God will get even with him."

I was about to say, "God doesn't always pay His debts." In my heart, I felt Uncle Pat was a decent, loving, and giving man, with flaws like the rest of us, but he certainly deserved better than he got.

Before I got a chance to speak, my mother shook her finger midair at no one as she often did when she ranted, "Maybe not is this life, but you rest assured, the Almighty will adjust the scales in the next life."

I couldn't argue. I'm Irish. We settle for that.

The Young Storyteller

The mile long walk from our house on Malden Street to the Abraham Lincoln school in Revere seemed like ten to a five-year old entering first grade. I had turned five that June in 1930, and officially, I was supposed to be at least five-and a-half by September to enter Revere schools; but I had a determined mother. She spent the month of August on the telephone talking to school officials.

"It's ridiculous for a child as smart and as prepared as my daughter to wait another year to begin her education. If we still lived in Boston, it would be no problem."

Somehow, she convinced them I was ready. I loved being the center of so much discussion, but looking back, I believe she may have oversold me.

The first few days my brother Frank, the only sibling out of seven still in elementary school, walked with me. Soon he left mornings without me, claiming I took too long. I knew he preferred to walk with his boy chums.

I can't imagine how my parents allowed me to walk alone, but there were no school buses in those days, nor did every family have two cars. Parents expected much of young children. Older children took care of younger ones without pay and we did real chores — not ones invented by parents to justify an allowance. Allowances were for rich kids.

So it was, lunch money knotted into my handkerchief inside my red pencil box, off I'd go, up Malden Street a half mile, turn left, and walk another half mile all by my skinny, little self. The trouble was, I had no conception of time. Anything by the side of the road captured my interest. I'd stop to pat a cat or a dog. I'd lean on fences and make faces at cows in a field. I'd pick up discarded roses that the local greenhouses used to throw away on their front lawn. A choice one would go to my teacher. My oldest sister, Marguerite, usually dressed me for school before she left for work. Her boyfriend drove by one day and saw me walking in a field knee high in grass picking golden rod. I wore a pink organdy dress she had just ironed that morning. He yelled to me to get going to school and I did.

When I got to school late, my homeroom teacher wouldn't let me in the class. She directed me to the principal's office where the late-arrival lady confronted me. I soon learned the drill. You had to stand outside the principal's office on one side of the door until the late-arrival lady came out. She could have been a secretary or a switchboard operator, but to a child all adults have power. She gave you the slip that allowed you to walk the corridor to your room. By now, the other children were settled in classrooms. I often got there after the Morning Prayer and Pledge of Allegiance.

Her voice was brimming with adult authority.

"Good morning, I am Miss Broadbent. Can you tell me why you are late this morning?" she said, peering over wire-rimmed glasses at my now disheveled clothes.

"I dunno," I replied first time it happened.

"Well, children cannot be late for school. You have to get to your class on time like all the other children. If you are late, you must have a good excuse or a note from your parents." She mentioned responsibility but I didn't even know what the word meant.

This not only happened once, but a couple of times a week. Soon, she seemed annoyed with me. Once or twice to my delight, another student waited with me, but my comrades in crime were less experienced and more scared. Since I had no good excuses, I was creative enough to make them up. Frankly, I had no idea why I was late. I was doing what was natural to a child who found the outdoor world more fascinating than school. Sometimes my daydreams slowed me down. I'd skip or dance on the dirt sidewalk imitating Jane Withers or Shirley Temple.

"My mother is very sick and I had to take care of baby Patrick and get him dressed," I heard myself saying the second time. I knew sickness and death were adult excuses for all sorts of things. At first, Miss Broadbent had felt sorry for me.

"Oh dear, I hope your mother is better soon," she'd say.

I used my mother's sickness at least three times, and I got so I believed it myself. Even found my eyes filled with tears on one occasion picturing my poor mother as really sick. Then I switched the blame to baby Patrick.

"He's only little and he spilt milk on me and I had to change my dress," I said, patting my dress. Another time I said he ran out of the house and I had to catch him.

Then I went back to my mother being sick. It seemed to work until the day of judgment arrived. I came home from school one day and my mother greeted me with hands on her hips.

"Is it not wonderful how a sick woman can get out of her bed, do three loads of wash, hang them on the line, then bake bread for her family?"

I ignored her and went on eating my jelly sandwich. I had no idea what she was getting at until she lifted my face and spoke.

"And what about the little brother who spilled milk all over his sister's dress and made her late for school?"

Then, I recognized the plot. It was mine.

"Do you realize how embarrassed I was when the school telephoned me to ask about my illness?" my mother said. "I was mortified that you would lie."

Well, I had to go bed that night right after supper. No radio for me. I could hear my parents talking downstairs in the kitchen when my father came home from work.

"Maybe the kid doesn't know the difference between a lie and the truth," my father said." Of course she does," my mother said. "And if she doesn't, its about time she learned. Go upstairs and talk to her."

My father sat at the foot of my bed.

"Why did you tell the teacher those lies about Mom and Patrick?"

"Because Miss Broadbent said I had to have an excuse. I could tell by her face that she meant what she said. So, I made up one. See, I don't have a watch so I never know the time." I held up my bony wrists to show their bareness. "Besides, even if I did have a watch, I can' t tell time very good. I only know my o'clocks not my half-pasts and all that stuff. I didn't know I was going to be late."

I started to sniffle. "Ma says I committed a mortal sin. I'm scared. Frank says if you die with a mortal sin on your soul you go straight to hell."

I knew mortal sins were bad. When my father would say "Jesus H. Christ," my mother scolded him. "It's a mortal sin to use the Lord's name in vain." Whenever my brothers complained about going to Mass on Sunday, she'd say, "Do you want to have a mortal sin on your soul?"

"I had to tell Miss Broadbent a lie so I could go to

my class. I didn't know it was a mortal sin." My father handed me his handkerchief.

"Maybe your mother exaggerated just to scare you. I'd say it was only a venial sin. That's not as big as a mortal sin. It's smaller," he said, "Easier for God to forgive".

"Whew," I said. Now I stopped the tears. All evening, I had pictured myself burning in hell. "Mom said mortal sins make black marks on my soul." My soul, I imagined, was a big-round pure-white circle somewhere behind my heart.

"Poor child," he said, rubbing my head. "Don't worry. Even some grownups tell a lie when the truth won't fit. But in this family we tell the truth and take the punishment. Don't worry about the little black spots on your soul. When you make your First Holy Communion the Holy Ghost will wash them all off. Of course, you have to tell the priest. Now say your prayers and tell God you're sorry for lying." He put the covers around my chin and kissed me. When he stood he said,

"And from now on never lie to Miss Broadbent."

"But how will I get to school on time?"

"We'll see to it that Frank walks with you until you're old enough to get there on time by yourself."

Before I fell asleep, I heard my parents arguing.

"Did you have to scare the crap out of the poor kid? And what's the matter with Frank that he can't wait a minute or two to walk his sister to school? I told you another year at home wouldn't hurt her."

"And forget everything the Sisters of Saint Joseph taught her in Charlestown. Not on your life. The nuns said she was ready for the first grade, and I trust them when it comes to education, not the likes of you. You never went to college."

Then I heard my father shout, "Frank, shut off the radio. Come here. I want to talk to you."

Problem solved. Poor Frank. He had his problems with me. His gait was short but quick and so every so often, he would have to stop until I caught up. His friends would go ahead without us. I managed to make him late one day. I stopped to make angels in a snow bank and he couldn't see me on the ground. He ran backwards right past me. He was furious when he found me. He told Miss Broadbent, it was my fault he was late. She looked at me and shook her head. I got detention and though he didn't, he still had to wait for me and walk me home from school.

By the end of that first year, I had made my own friends. Now I walked to school with them and I always got there on time.

When I was seven and made my First Holy Communion and learned the Act of Contrition. After I said it, I pictured the Holy Ghost scrubbing all those black spots off my soul. Free and pure, I vowed I'd stop making up stories. But those old venial sins didn't go away easily. For years afterward, every time I told a story or passed on information, I'd get the same response.

"You're making it up," my brothers or sisters would say as they walked away in disgust. Or my mother would narrow her eyes and ask, "Are you sure that really happened?" They questioned everything I said, and with my luck, I drew Miss Broadbent for a home-room teacher in the second grade.

Nickel Day at Revere Beach

"Can we go, Ma? Can we? Pul-eeze" We nagged her the minute we spotted the ad in the Boston Daily Record for "NICKEL DAY AT REVERE BEACH".

The time was the 1930's shortly after the stock market crash numbed the country and threw Americans into breadlines. My father out of work, my mother never said, yes. She said, maybe, or we'll see. I guess she never knew in advance if she would have enough money when the day arrived.

Usually, we only went to Revere Beach on extraordinarily hot days. And then only to swim. Like automobiles and single-family houses, amusement rides were not an option for us; they were for the rich. But one day in summer, parents like mine could afford to put their children on amusements, and that was Nickel Day. My two brothers and I spent days anticipating its arrival.

Weeks before, we, the three youngest in a family of eight, cleaned our rooms, emptied trash, and faced the dreaded chore of washing dishes for ten people without the usual harangue. When our mother said, "You'll have to be good," we complied. How she must have pinched pennies before Nickel Day arrived. Carfare to and from the beach and $3.00 spent for our three strips of five-cent tickets would have bought a lot of bread and milk in the thirties.

The crescent shaped beach was crowded most summer days, but my parents' priority wasn't to entertain us, it was to feed us and keep us healthy. So, our young lives were narrow. We didn't have the entertainment options children have today. For us, swimming in fluorescent waves cresting high above our heads was a rare and exhilarating experience. The waves traveled at a speed that made them deliciously frightening. We stiffened our small skinny bodies into boards; then with arms outstretched held close to our ears, we dove fearlessly. The ocean's momentum hurled us onto the sandy beach. On Nickel Day, that special treat was merely the beginning.

After we swam, we devoured a home-packed lunch. One day all my mother had to fill sandwiches with were baked beans. I can see her slapping mayonnaise on their ugly brownness.

"I'm not going to eat those," I said turning up my nose.

"You don't have to. You can go without," she said.

After a couple of hours in the ocean the bean sandwiches tasted like roast beef. But food was secondary. We devoured lunch in huge bites to get across the street where action awaited.

Across from the beach on the boulevard, every amusement ride popular in the thirties lined the sidewalk: Roller Coaster, Ferris Wheel, the Whip, Dodgem cars, and for the less courageous - the Flying Horses. Neon lights, garish green, red, and yellow splashed faces of the good-time crowd. Food vendors hawked their wares competitively and constantly. Their makeshift stands exuded aromas of hamburger and onions frying. Skeet ball operators held up stuffed animals to tempt you to try your luck. The fun house teased you indoors with a mirrored sample of your distorted self. For hours, we stood amused by the mere making of cotton candy or salt water taffy. What was not to love?

On one Nickel Day, to get to the beach, the four of us stood all the way in a hot crowded bus, wearing itchy wool bathing suits that chafed your inner thighs. When we got off the bus on Broadway behind the amusements, my mother took a deep breath.

"Just smell that salt air," she said. She carried a large shopping bag that held lunch and the white bed sheet that would serve as our changing tent later. We each toted clean underwear and a towel in a paper bag. By now, my Mother's forehead and the underarms of her button-down-the-front calico dress were wet with perspiration. She trudged up the small hill as she ushered the three of us toward the beach. At the top, she stopped, took several deep breaths.

"Close your eyes, children. Listen to the sound of

the ocean. Stop and thank God for His gifts. Feel the breeze. Isn't this exciting?"

Exciting? I silently questioned my mother's credibility. The ocean was okay, but how could it compare to the music of the nickelodeon, the food smells, and the glitzy amusements that superseded anything in nature? I wanted to shout, let's hurry up and swim, eat lunch, then get to the good part; the amusements. It wasn't until years later than I understood my mother's feelings.

I assumed Revere Beach would remain spectacular. As a married adult, I had moved to Maine, and on a trip home, when my husband and I went to Revere beach, I discovered I had lost the recreational Mecca of my childhood. Regrettably, the drug culture that overtook our country in the sixties did not stop when it reached my beach. Absent were the families with small children. A younger, undisciplined, crowd stalked the boulevard looking for trouble. Amusement facades were violated with graffiti. Beer bottles, soda cans and food wrappings were everywhere. Many of the amusements were not operating. Pastel colored one-room shingled cottages that once stood on grassy patches beside or behind the amusements now displayed "For Sale" signs. The men and women, who once leisurely sat on their stoops watching people, had gone inside. As my mother so aptly stated, "Revere Beach has gone to seed". The ocean had supposedly become polluted.

Other economic and social changes affected the beach. By the mid-sixties, the average family owned a car or two, or perhaps a recreational vehicle that now glutted highways to Cape Cod, Maine, or New Hampshire on weekends. Others moved to the suburbs and spent weekends barbecuing around pools in their backyards.

Soon, the booths were boarded up. The roller coaster and other rides were dismantled. The small cottages were razed. Sheer nostalgia helped a few eating places escape the bulldozer's shovel after real estate developers grabbed the ocean front property. Today, there is no music tinkling from the merry-go-round, or delicious smells emanating from food stands. On the boulevard, where the amusements and eating-places once flourished, now stand high-rise brick and cement condominium buildings. Stark, gray clusters of windowed columns shoot upward, reminding me of an isolated space city in one of Isaac Asminov's novels.

The air is still salt laden. Smooth water-washed rocks are still plentiful. The waves still speak in roars at high tide. Since daughters have a way of becoming their mothers, I know what my mother meant, as these days nature feeds my senses. Now at Revere Beach, I inhale the ocean air, run the sand through my fingers, marvel at the artistry of stones and shells. The sands of memory shift but precious childhood memories remain fixed.

I can feel and see myself staring impatiently across the boulevard at childish delights. My mother sits on a bench in the shade of a long gazebo that faces the ocean and beach, her laced oxfords surrounded by our messy beach bags. Frank, the oldest, has gone to buy our tickets. When he returns, she tears them apart, and mutters.

"I suppose this is foolish, we'll have nothing to show for our money."

I'm old enough to notice my mother is getting tired. Up since six, when she made doughnuts for my brother John to sell to strangers, her dark Irish eyes sparkle as she hands us each our tickets.

"Calm down, and stay with your brothers," she says to me.

"You watch your giddy sister now," she yells to Frank as we cross the boulevard. She will sit on the gazebo bench and wait until we return.

I remember how I fingered the coiled, pink, perforated strip of cardboard. A dollar's worth of nickel tickets — twenty options — rides, games, food. What would it be, a Kohr's® custard or a ride on the Dodgems®? It was all at my fingertips. The incredible power of choice was mine! On Nickel Day at Revere Beach, a skinny little girl felt rich and spoiled.

It was a bargain that lasted a lifetime.

Pies and Parents

My Irish mother, may God rest her soul, was a terrible cook. Our Sunday dinner, potatoes, vegetables thrown in a pot and boiled with either spareribs, brown corned beef, or smoked shoulder, was her version of gourmet cooking. Her pot roast, a rarity in our large family, was cooked until it was the taste and texture of a cinder block. She never broiled steak; she fried it until it curled and turned gray. Thanks to what I call, the Natural Laws of Compensation, my mother was an exceptional pastry cook and baker.

Maggie's piecrust was as flaky as a French croissant. Her yeast bread was worthy of Fannie Farmer's envy. I have yet to taste a doughnut that equaled the ones she cut by hand and dropped into hot bubbly grease from the end of a long tine fork. The residue of these, I suspect, line my arteries to this day. This talent was Godsend when my father lost his job in 1937. With five children still at home, and since my father was too proud to apply for public assistance, she started baking goods to sell.

I was ten, or maybe eleven, when I ran around our congested Somerville neighborhood pulling a red wagon lined with pies. My mother paid me a nickel for each pie I sold, and another nickel upon delivery. I was delighted, as for ten cents, I could see a movie. In those days, an eleven-year-old did not baby-sit. Mothers "minded" each other's children without fee.

Although my father owned a car, I was my mother's designated delivery girl because my father said he was too busy looking for a job. Employed or unemployed, my father was excused from similar chores under the guise of gender. Despite his flaws, his children felt responsible for making him feel like a man in the face of my mother's competence. Sensitivity was considered a feminine attribute, financial management a masculine talent.

"Busy looking for a job, my foot," my mother said, carefully wrapping a pie in waxed paper. "Your father has false pride, that's the problem."

"What's the difference between real pride and false pride?" I asked.

"Pride, my dear girl, is what I feel when I look at those pies lined up on the pantry shelf. Look at them. Don't they look like pictures?"

My mother was right. They looked mouth watering delicious, but I couldn't attest to their quality because I seldom got to eat her products once she started baking for strangers.

We would come home from school ravenous. The

kitchen burst with the aroma of apples and spices. Luscious looking lemon meringue pies lined the pantry shelves. Crocks full of plump doughnuts beckoned from crystal jars. Her instructions were: "Fill up on bread and apple butter and then you each can have one doughnut from the crock with the red cover." The crock with the red cover was the place for stale, deformed or broken doughnuts.

I managed to market within the confines of our street. Pies were our biggest seller. Especially on holidays. We lived in a congested city neighborhood where the more prosperous neighbors bought their homemade doughnuts and pies daily. But at a price of twenty-five to sixty cents for pies, even the poor could afford to indulge their families after a holiday or Sunday meal.

Fearing my mother's acid tongue, my father dared not say he resented the fact that she never baked for the family. Instead, he said how lucky the neighbors were or he'd tinge his remarks with sarcasm.

"Do you fill my apple pies that full, Margaret?" or "That's a fine glaze you got on that crust. Just like the glaze on the last pie you made for me. Two years ago, was it, my love?" My mother would just glare at him.

One afternoon, Mrs. Larson left a note on her tenement door telling me to deliver her pie the following day.

"Their government check probably didn't arrive," my mother said. Mr. Larson worked on the highway for the Work Project Administration.

"Put it in the refrigerator and take it by tomorrow after the mail is delivered," she added.

After supper that night, my mother went to the adult session of the mission the Franciscans were giving in our city parish. Movies were not her thing. Missions, novenas, and prayer were what helped my mother cope with reality.

My father, two brothers, and I were playing Michigan Rummy around the oil-clothed table under the nautical styled pin up lamp I had picked out. It had a wrought iron base shaped like a ship's anchor. The white paper shade was sprinkled with tiny red and blue anchors that matched the boats on the oilcloth. The light focused on the table and put the rest of the kitchen into soft darkness so you couldn't see the tired, unmatched furniture and shabby linoleum.

Our white-gray mongrel dog, Rover, our family food disposal, was always under that table. Whenever we gathered there, the dog thought we were going to eat. He'd sit forever waiting for crumbs or leftovers that never came.

"I'm starved," my father said. "Let's eat the pie." Mischief dotted his soft blue eyes.

"What pie?" young Patrick asked.

"He means the one in the refrigerator. Ma made it to sell to Mrs. Larson. Ma would kill us if we touched it," I protested. Everyone at the table shot me a "you pain in the ass" glance.

"She'll bake her another. A nice fresh one. For the love of Pete, when do we ever get to eat anything she makes," my father said.

My brother Frank opened the refrigerator. "It's lemon meringue!" he said, as if he had discovered uranium. Frank and I exchanged a furtive look. We didn't jump at the opportunity at first.

My father wouldn't let up.

"It'll be worth her wrath," he prodded.

When the saliva started to accumulate in my mouth, it didn't take much convincing. Once again, I looked at Frank, then my father. Surely we'd catch the devil. I pondered how much protection my father had to offer. Then I didn't care. We arrived at risk simultaneously.

"Patrick, you take the first piece," my father said.

"She never gets mad at you." Her ten-year-old baby was still able to get away with more than the rest of us. In no time, the four of us were devouring the pie.

"Leave one piece." my father said, holding up one finger. We all assumed it was for our mother.

My mother came home from church in a great mood and joined us in the parlor. We all sat relaxed listening to the radio. She never went near the kitchen. By now, we had digested and forgotten Mrs. Larson's pie.

The following day, I sauntered into the kitchen for breakfast. I heard the clunk of the wooden rolling pin coming from the pantry. My mother was making pie crust. Rover came into the kitchen to sit under the table as I ate. My mother whipped around the corner, her hands and apron covered with flour. My heart skipped when I saw her face.

"Get that bloody dog out of here before I whack him." Her white floured hands clutched the kitchen broom.

"Why? What did he do?" I stood in front of Rover to protect him. Glad I wasn't the object of her anger, but nervous about being in the line of fire.

"He ate Mrs. Larson's pie. I woke up this morning and the pie plate was on the floor."

"Oh?" I said, and with that, I could feel my face turn scarlet.

"Just a minute." Her eyes narrowed. She gave me one of her bone dissolving looks. I could never lie to my mother. "Your father told me that Patrick opened the refrigerator door and the pie fell out, and before he could get to it, Rover ate the whole pie. Is that true?"

I bowed my head in silence.

"Jaaack," she screamed loudly, though my father was sitting close by in the dining room.

Hail Mary

My parents never put up our Christmas tree until their young children were sound asleep on Christmas Eve. How they managed still puzzles me. Where had they hid it? I still don't know. But, thanks to their trickery, my childhood Christmas mornings were exhilarating.

The fresh smell of pine as we rushed down the stairs from our bedrooms meant Santa had come. He got credit for both tree and gifts. These days, plastic trees and decorations go up after Halloween in the stores, and right after Thanksgiving in households. Decorations become fixtures, as in-place as the kitchen table, stove or plastic flowers. Christmas traditions, like people, have changed. In pre-World War II days, Christmas was a holy day not just another holiday.

On the first of the four Sundays of Advent, we began preparing ourselves for the Feast of Christmas. The Advent wreath was placed in the middle of the dining room table every Sunday at dinner, we said a few prayers and a chosen child added a purple candle: except for the third week, Gaudete Sunday, when pink candles were used to say, "Rejoice, the Lord is coming." Each burning candle brought us closer to Christ's birthday.

What I remember most was my family's unusual Advent rite. I've never met anyone, outside of my family, clergy or layperson, who ever did what we did.

Four weeks before Christmas, on the first day of Advent, we started saying Hail Mary's — and, Dear God, we said a lot of them.

At some novena or mission my mother attended, she learned that if you said three thousand Hail Mary's between the beginning of Advent and Christmas Eve, you would get anything you wished for at Christmas. Looking back, I wonder if she invented the idea just to keep us quiet on long winter nights. Margaret, Frank, Patrick, and I were not only silent, we were so busy counting and praying we hadn't a moment to listen to the radio or fight.

Scraps of paper bearing our names and progress littered the house. A mark for four Hail Mary's, then a diagonal slash written through these for our fifth. Official Hail Mary records were kept upstairs in our bedrooms, but downstairs, on the paper the meat came in, or on the back of a school paper, we kept temporary but transferable records. The Hail Mary race became as competitive as stickball.

"You can pray anywhere," my mother said, "Even while you're getting dressed or eating. The Blessed Virgin is always listening." The deal in Catholicism was you could always pray to God, but you also could get God's attention by going through His sweet, understanding Mother, the Blessed Virgin, of whom, it was said, had lots of pull.

"How many did you say today?" I'd ask Frank. Frank was the family brain. He had figured out how many he needed to say per hour, day, or week.

"Five Hundred," he'd answer, prompting me to speed up. To this day, I can say a rosary in nanoseconds.

Harry, the family wise guy, laughed at us. He went out with his friends to shoot pool.

"You suckers are only gonna get what they can afford to give us no matter how hard you pray."

Judicious Margaret, nine years older than I, was hot in the holy race with the rest of us. Since she wasn't skeptical, I had faith.

We believers would sit around the kitchen table every night after supper praying like Carmelite nuns. We watched each other's lips and pencils move like sleuths on a case.

The first year I met the Hail Mary requirements, having said all three thousand, I got what I asked for on Christmas morning: a porcelain doll with eyes that opened and closed. There were extra gifts I hadn't asked for like those fat little storybooks I loved, as well as paper dolls, crayons and coloring books. Expectations weren't high in the late thirties. A child's Christmas list was short. Instead of toys in our stockings, we found oranges, apples, nuts, or hard candy covered with stocking lint. Fruit, a luxury in winter, was relished.

By the third year, I stopped saying Hail Mary's when I reached 1,000 because, unaware of our family practice, one of the nuns gave our class a lecture on praying slowly with meaning and respect. Since I couldn't slow down my Hail Mary's, I quit. I was too young to realize mixed messages were part of the Catholic clerical authority.

Shortly before Christmas that year, my father was laid off. My mother voiced her concern at the breakfast table as she thumbed through the newspaper ads.

"Jack, where on God's earth will we get money for Christmas presents? Patrick still believes in Santa."

"Like you say, Mag, God will provide," he answered, but his face clouded in concern.

"Don't worry about me," I told them brimming with pre-teen heroics. "All I want is a pair of tugboat shoes." They were the rage that year, squared toe, laced sporty shoes with sponge soles. I played hard so I always needed shoes.

They took me at my word. Christmas morning, along side a stocking filled with the usual fruit and candy treats, was a pair of knee socks and a tan pair of square toed tugboat shoes with dark brown laces. And that was all! I refused to count a hateful pair of multi-colored mittens Margaret knitted to use up yarn scraps. She marked them, "To Rose from Santa". Maybe deep down I expected my heroics to improve my bounty.

Feeling cheated and angry, I rifled through everyone's gifts discovering no one, except, Patrick, who still believed in Santa, got so-called good stuff (nonessentials) that Christmas. I can't remember their gifts — just mine. Part of me was a hurt child, but I must have been on the cusp of growing up, because I never mentioned my disappointment to my parents.

Besides, in my heart, I knew I deserved what I got. Two thousand more Hail Mary's and things might have been a lot different.

My Influential Aunt

I think it was John Updike who said, "Every choice is an exclusion." The words gave me pause when I read them. I assume that was how my mother felt when I spent summer vacations at my Aunt Nora's house as a child.

"Aunt Nora says I can stay longer. Is that okay with you?" I said on the phone, "I love being here."

"I think you love your Aunt more than you love me," my mother said. "You've been gone two weeks." I felt so guilty, I prayed to the Virgin Mary to help me love my mother more. Truth was, I loved them both — each in different ways — but children are inclined to believe whatever their mother's tell them.

Neither my mother nor aunt were women who cuddled you, at least not that I remember, but, secretly, I did wish my mother had her sister's phlegmatic disposition. Young as I was, I realized my mother had much more to cope with than my aunt. With seven children still at home, four of them teenagers, my mother yelled to keep her sanity. Soft-spoken Aunt Nora contrasted favorably.

For whenever I was around, she never raised her voice. Most of all, I loved her because, like a cape-less superwoman in a comic strip, she showed up just in time. Always, when I needed her most.

My father's success moved us from Avon Place in Charlestown to a finer house on the outskirts of Boston in then rural Revere. To our relatives, it was a show-place. To my immediate family, well, I'm not so sure.

Isolated from relatives and neighbors, my reluctant playmates were two brothers. My date of birth squeezed me between them. Frank, older, got attention for his talents. Patrick, the youngest in our family, like most three-years-olds, was charismatic. Everyone's life could go on nicely if I never existed. I was rail skinny, and constantly scolded for ankle socks that, through no fault of mine, kept disappearing into my shoes. Patrick liked me okay, but I knew he preferred playing boy stuff with Frank. Maybe sensitivity exaggerates my memory, but in those days, Frank tolerated me as one tolerates a migraine. Blonde, ringlet-capped three-year-old Patrick sponged up every visitor's attention, including Aunt Nora's. No wonder I felt unworthy when I overheard her discussing me with my mother on a Sunday visit.

"How awful the boys leave her out," my aunt said to my mother as I listened, sitting on the stairs outside the kitchen screen door. I read and watched as my brothers played ball with my three male cousins in the back yard.

"She gets to play when they have no one else," my mother said. "Good thing she likes to read."

"She reads because she's lonely. Let her come stay with me for a spell. The change will do her good."

It's not as if Aunt Nora ever doted on me. If she had the means to dote, her four sons would have been the recipients. She made me feel special. Maybe I was the daughter she never had.

For a few weeks every summer for the next three years, Aunt Nora squeezed me into the small, five-room cold-water flat she shared with husband Harry and their four sons. I slept on a cot in the dining room. They had no bathtub, just a pull chain toilet and sink. Everyone showered weekly, or as needed, at the Boys or Girls Club of Boston where a quarter included soap and towel.

"You're nuts to leave breezy Revere for the hot asphalt of Charlestown," my cousin Charlie said, but I didn't think so. Revere was truck farmer country. They grew vegetables and hogs, not children. Allston Street was teeming with children my age. Not only that, Aunt Nora asked my opinion on what to wear or what she should make the boys for lunch.

Flanked with three-family houses on both sides, to a child of eight, Allston Street was what the Las Vegas strip must be to a gambler — the place was alive with action. City children played fast moving games like Ring-Alevo, Kick the Can, and Red Light. In Charlestown, I was one of the clan. In our Italian neighborhood in Revere, my family was the Irish family who ate fruit and vegetables from cans and soft doughy Wonder bread. I had one playmate, Gloria Del Russo, who worked her father's farm and had little playtime. If the North End of Boston was the Italian ghetto, Charlestown was the Irish-American ghetto. In those days, first-generation immigrants lived where they were comfortable — among each other. I didn't know where the Lutherans, Baptists, Episcopalians and Jews lived in Charlestown. I never knew any.

Despite my gender, my cousins, Charlie, Brud, Joe and Billy, treated me, as we would say then, swell. Joe and I, born the same year, had a special bond. Blonde, sturdy as a rock, dark brown eyes, he had a face as pleasant as a sunflower. Now deceased, Joe surely grins and says to everyone in Heaven "Hi ya, where ya from?" in a wonderful flat Boston accent.

Wherever Joe went on those summer days, he took me along. We dog paddled in the oil-slicked waters of the Mystic River and I kept the unnecessary score as he played ball with his friends at the Neck in Sullivan Square by the old Schrafft's chocolate factory. Together we walked up Allston to Bunker Hill Street to get butter and eggs at Kennedy's Butter and Egg Store for Aunt Nora, and Lucky Strikes at Nick's Variety for Uncle Harry. (In thirty years, those cigarettes would destroy my Uncle's voice box before they took his life).

"Is that your girl, Joey?" my cousin Joe's friends teased as we walked to movies at Thompson Square. It didn't phase Joe.

"Nah, she's my cousin Rosie from Revere." A ten-cent movie a week was part of my Aunt's vacation package. Movies were a rarity in Revere.

Boys, I soon discovered, had lots more fun than girls did. Home in Revere, Gloria and I cut out paper dolls — and that was okay — but my adrenaline didn't pump as it did when I played city games. I remember saying, "oh shit" to impress the boys, but my neck and face flushed when Joe's face registered disapproval.

My cousins attended St. Frances de Sales parochial school, where I had gone to kindergarten before we moved to Revere. They served as altar boys so Aunt Nora spent half her life washing, starching, and ironing acolyte whites. I can see ten-year-old Joe rolling out of bed, rubbing his eyes at 5:30 a.m. when the Big Ben alarm clock shrilled so he could serve Mass at six. The next day it would be one of the older boys, Charlie, or Brud, and one day, when old enough, little Billy would serve.

After supper, we'd all sit on the stoop playing Fish or Old Maid until the sun went down. Allowed to stay up until small bedrooms cooled, we lit thin rails of punk to keep mosquitoes away. The heated discussions began when the adults came out after the nightly news radio broadcast.

"I don't care if he is a thief, he takes care of his own," one neighbor said when James Michael Curley's name was defamed.

"Maybe Roosevelt is an isolationist but I think he's right to stay out of Europe's business. And I'll be damned, half of us wouldn't be eating, if it weren't for him."

Politicians were either heroes or devils in their eyes, and despite what the powerful assumed, the poor were uneducated but not stupid.

"You said a mouthful, O' Reilly, I'm with you," another woman chimed in, her elbows leaning on windowsills. Women were too tired to deal with three flights of stairs on hot nights. Through the soft summer air they held conversations with each other or shouted below to correct their respective husband's statements.

Saturday nights, Aunt Nora gave us money so we could walk down to Medford Street to a yeast-smelling bakery. At 9:00 p.m., the hot doughnuts for the next day were plucked from bubbling hot fat. Five cents bought us each two plump jelly doughnuts fresher than sunrise. I drooled as much from the smell as the taste.

I felt I was on a pedestal, but a corn chowder incident taught me Aunt Nora made all her children feel as important as she did me.

"Ugh. This chowder tastes funny," Joe said one Friday night at the supper table.

"Like soap," Billy added.

Never to hurt my dear aunt's feelings, I kept quiet, forced down the chowder. So did Charlie and Brud, the older boys.

"Your father works hard to put a square meal on the table. Stop complaining and eat your supper," Aunt Nora said. She served Uncle Harry mackerel and because the children hated fish, she fed us corn chowder.

Later, when Joe and I were washing the dishes, he found a pink bar of Lifebouy soap stuck on the inside bottom of the blue enamel chowder pot. Aunt Nora was in the parlor reading the paper.

"Look, Mum." He tipped the pot so she could see.

"What's that?" she said, removing reading glasses from her blue-gray eyes. "Oh kids," she said, putting her hand to her mouth in horror. "I bet it fell from the soap dish when I rinsed the pan." Her face folded into regret. "I should've listened. I'm so sorry."

An adult apologizing? I was dumbfounded. When my mother got mad at herself, she managed to blame us. Aunt Nora gave us each three cents to buy a slush, and we joked about bubbles in the toilet for days.

The summer before I entered the sixth grade, my father lost his job and our house in Revere. My parents moved to a flat in Somerville, the city next to Charlestown. Vacations with Aunt Nora were behind me, but now she visited often.

Entering Junior High, I complained in her presence to my mother that I had nothing decent to wear.

"Maggie," she scolded, "For God's sake, don't you remember how awful it was for us going to school in shabby clothes?"

"And just where do you think I'll get the money?" my mother asked, with her shoulder chip in place.

"Borrow it from the Morris Plan. Pay it back twenty-five or fifty cents a week. I'm as poor as you, but my boys look spiffy when they go off to school or Sunday

Mass. How do you think I do it?"

Terrified of debt, my mother figured interest rates too fast to buy into a loan company. She'd never spend what she didn't have.

I knew my mother tried. One Saturday she came home from downtown Boston with a package for me. I had begged her for a reversible coat like my girlfriends in school were wearing — loose fitting with raglan sleeves, gabardine twill raincoat on one side, tweed, or wool plaid on the other. Then it was the ultimate sporty statement worn with plaid skirts, sloppy joe sweaters and brown and white saddle shoes. Most of which I didn't own, but a coat flung casually over my shoulders, as I walked from class to class, would hide this fact.

"I bought you your coat." My mother grinned triumphantly handing me a huge gray Filene's Basement box. I opened it with gratitude and anticipation, but my face fell when I removed the tissue. From the coat's fabric side a red, green, black and predominantly orange plaid screamed at me. Not only that, it was the wrong style: puffed sleeves and a belt. I was not the puffed sleeve type. I stood fixed and speechless.

"I can't wear it." My stomach whirred as I spoke.

"Why not? Try it on. It's your size." Her eyes were quizzical, demanding.

"I hate it. You'll have to take it back." My mother's expression was unprecedented. She pulled her head back as if I had just slapped her face.

"It's what you asked for," she shouted. "Reversible gabardine on one side, wool on the other."

"I'm sorry. I hate it." I wanted to take the damn coat, throw it on the floor, and step on it and scream, "It's awful." To say I hated it took courage enough.

"You'll wear it or you'll get none. Put it back in the box," she yelled, before her mouth rested in that thin-lipped angry face she shaped so precisely.

Aunt Nora stopped by for tea around three o'clock that afternoon. I sat in the dining room doing my homework. In the kitchen, unaware I was still home, the sisters chatted about corns and swollen feet. My mother related her morning outing. She had taken the subway to Boston, gone to Mass in town, then rifled through Filene's Basement and came upon a wonderful buy on coat for Rose. "I'll show you," I heard her say, "It's not quite her style so she wants me to take it back, but she'll wear it. I'll see to that."

After a rustle of cardboard and tissue, I heard Aunt Nora's voice.

"Mother of God, Maggie, you want our Rosie to wear that thing. Old man McIver's horse wore a blanket prettier than that coat!" McIver was their milkman in Cambridge after they arrived from Ireland.

My mother didn't respond.

"Take the bloody thing back. It's no bargain at five dollars. I wouldn't take it for free." My aunt was never loud but her tone was emphatic. I knew my mother respected her sister's opinion. I wanted to rush into the next room and hug Aunt Nora. The coat would go back.

I never mentioned the coat again nor did my mother or my aunt, but my mother was no longer angry. Later, I earned money at F.W.Woolworth's after school and on Saturdays, and bought myself a camel's hair coat. A reversible coat would have been an affront to my mother's taste. It didn't matter. The ugly plaid coat had served its purpose. Thanks to Aunt Nora's influence, I knew I deserved a better coat and I managed to get one.

Fashionable Frannie

When I was thirteen, some of the girls in junior high tweezed their eyebrows, but my very, very, best friend, Frannie, not only tweezed her eyebrows, she tweezed her hairline straight across her forehead.

"How do I look?" Frannie asked one day when we met to walk to school together at the corner of Pearl and Perkins Street.

"Great outfit," I responded.

Plaid skirt, sloppy joe sweater, and penny loafers were the clothes we used to offend our parents back then. She always dressed better than I did. Three children in her family — eight in mine.

"No, silly. I mean my face. Does it look longer? More oval?"

She had to point out that she shaved, then plucked an inch or more of her hairline before I knew what she was talking about.

"That must have hurt awful," I said. Just once, she had attempted to pluck my eyebrows and one pluck was enough. My eyebrows bush to this day.

Frannie constantly complained about what she called her pumpkin face. This friend knew what she needed to hear, so I stood back examining her with believable scrutiny.

"Yeah, you're right. Your face does look longer, much thinner."

Our friendship was cemented by an age-old rule: one girlfriend was obliged to convince the other she was not ugly. With Frannie's petite frame, small waist and ample bosom, my job should have been a cinch.

"Look in the mirror," I'd say on afternoons we got together to swap clothes and talk about boys. "You're gorgeous." Brown hair, streaked with blonde highlights: transparent, blue, quarter-sized eyes with lashes as long as a llama's, it surprised me she needed convincing.

Too tall for boys my age, underweight and flat chested, it was a tough sell convincing me I wasn't ugly. My brothers called me "Six o'clock", and kidded me about going down the drain in the bathtub. Mousy brown hair, indefinite bluish eyes, with a relentless case of acne that broadcasted my adolescent turmoil, I felt a misfit. But dear Frannie helped me belong. She claimed I did the same for her.

Frannie taught me lots. Not only things like how to floor-wax my penny loafers so I didn't have to polish them, but how to jitterbug and talk to boys.

"Ask them questions about themselves," Frannie said, her broomstick skirt swishing as we jitterbugged together. "I read in Cosmopolitan that men like that." She used the word men, but we only knew boys. Boys who lived on our street. Boys who leaped like gazelles when their mothers called them for supper.

She and her younger sister Marie convinced me God wouldn't strike all three of us dead if we played hooky and went to Boston's Metropolitan Theater to hear Sinatra, Dorsey, James, the Duke or other big names. We'd save our lunch money, cash a few Hood's milk bottles and hop on the Boston Elevated subway, praying no one we knew would be on the train.

"I'll have to lie if my mother asks me about school." I said.

"That's okay. Tell it in confession and add a rosary to the penance Father Foley gives you, that's all," her sister Marie said.

"God will understand. He loves music too," Frannie added, "The angels are always blowing trumpets or playing harps." Confession or not, though I was riddled with guilt for my truancy, to this day I cherish the memory of those dazzling performances.

Best of all, Frannie insisted I was the Lauren-Bacall type and used her cosmetic skill to shape me. She set my hair in a pageboy and covered my pimples with Max Factor's No. 2 pancake make-up. Tangee's Red Hot lipstick from Woolworth's Five and Dime sizzled my lips. A hair-flinging starlet while at school, I scrubbed my face raw before coming home. That's when I graduated from the uglies to the ultimate —

boys. No wonder our friendship lasted.

Dramatically serious about Mass, Missions, and Novenas, we were not beyond imitating old Father Foley's waddle and brogue. Church took a chunk of time out of our adolescent lives, and we'd never pass a church, or hear the name Jesus, without bowing our heads.

Our genes infused with Irish wit and humor, in high school we were invited to join social clubs like the Merry Makers because we were a comedic twosome. No mean teacher was left unscathed. "Holy Moly! Here comes Margoli," we'd say to our classmates when a huge breasted teacher who always wore a loose fitting bra walked down the hall. Our English teacher, who felt she was hired to teach only the bright kids, was a crank with a bad overbite, we named "Beaver Johnson." Our math teacher, who had one leg short-ened in an auto accident, but who had a preponder-ance for brushing against our nubile soft spots was called "Limp the Pimp."

The chess club, the debating society, or the chorus, were for other kids. We called them squares. Frannie wanted to be a vocalist with a band — now that was cool. "Cool" had the same connotation as it has today.

Friday or Saturday nights, because of Frannie's ambition, we'd sneak to dances at the Raymor/ Playmor ballrooms on Huntington Avenue in Boston to hear swing bands. There we met an amateur prizefighter named Pretzie who yelled across the floor to anyone we danced with.

"She's a good girl. Watch your step. Or answer to me. Yah hear." One look at our defender, and our dance partner disappeared for the next set. How frustrating to know a real live prizefighter and not be able to brag to my brothers.

If and when we did meet a boy we liked, he took us to a movie, put his arm around us in the dark. The aggressive ones attempted to kiss us at the front door of our house at the end of the night. We couldn't get into trouble as we went everywhere by subway, streetcar or bus. Frannie and I told each other everything. Boys, not sex, were the topic of most conversations. "Doing it" was not within the realm of possibilities for us. We were lucky we even knew about "It".

After high school, Frannie and I obtained what our parents called "white collar" jobs working in an office. Our parents were proud. Their generation of Irish worked in factories, or as domestics, or did manual labor. We dressed in high heels, silk stockings, tailored suits, rayon or silk dresses and always wore a hat and gloves to work.

As we got older, instead of going to the movies on Sunday, we took the El into Boston's Ken Club where we nursed cokes and listened while jazz musicians sat in and jammed. We'd slap hands with white and black musicians, saying, "Hi ya, Man give me some skin," or "What's your latest gig, Man?" When I think of it now, our greetings were as corny as the Mason Lodge's handshake or the golfers', "How ya hitting 'em." People do and say silly things just to belong.

We never drank alcohol, swore, or did the unmentionable, and with all our innocence, we were considered "hep chicks". We read Downbeat Magazine and could name every musician in all the big name bands. Frannie dated Jack, a trumpet player with Red Norvo's band. Jack promised to get her an audition as a vocalist with a band, but he was drafted. He was killed in action overseas.

I never told Frannie I didn't think she could sing. Carry a tune maybe, but no tonal quality or range. I had a better voice than she did, but when it came to looks, she was a younger version of Angela Lansbury, so she caught a few auditions with bands. Nothing materialized. Her disappointment was mine. I also never told her that I thought her ambition shallow. My lofty sights were set on teaching or journalism. My mother said, if she had any money, which she didn't, that she would spend it sending her sons to college.

"You're only going to get married and have a bunch of kids," were her words — endorsed by my father, and many other parents of women in that generation.

When I told Fran, she was visibly upset.

"You're smart, Ro. You belong in college." I could tell she was sincere. We were close. She knew the dysfunctions, real and imagined, of my family. I knew hers. Not too many people knew her mother divorced her father and had remarried outside of the Church. Divorce was behind-curtain-talk in Irish-Catholic circles. I thought she told me, her very best friend, everything. That was until one Friday night.

I stopped by her house to pick her up. On Wednesday nights, we went to the Broadway Theatre to get the free gold embossed china for the hope chest neither of us ever owned.

"Let's go into the living room. I've something to tell you before we leave," she said. "Sit down. This will bowl you over." I sat on her mother's chintz covered chair.

"I am going away," she paused. Using her flair for drama, she cast her llama lashed eyes downward. "I'll be leaving a week from Saturday to enter the Sisters of Saint Joseph's."

Her declaration jolted me. Then I remembered phone calls she never shared the contents of, a cryptic conversation with her mother. I thought it had to do with her sister Marie or her brother. Getting into the convent, in those days, was like getting a job in high-tech in Massachusetts during the early nineties. It wasn't easy. Frannie? The convent? No way! I'd have been a more likely candidate. At least I read the Archdiocese newspaper, the Pilot, fed the poor on Thanksgiving and Christmas with the Sodality of St. John of God, and I worked for Monsignor Wright's Propagation of the Faith.

"Because of my mother's divorce and re-marriage," Frannie said, "the Order suggested no fanfare be made of my acceptance. I must serve in the Archdiocese of Florida where my background won't be an issue."

In the few days before she left, I cried often, but pretended I thought it was wonderful that God had chosen her. Inside, I felt betrayed. How could she do this to me? I forced laughter at her going away party when Frannie, the fashion plate, modeled the long bloomers, petticoats, and cotton black dress she would be required to wear in the convent.

Frannie's departure left a big gap. It took a while to make new friends. Not one jazz enthusiast among them. I took courses at night. I even interviewed for a job in Washington, D.C. We corresponded faithfully. Her letters became very nun-like. She was "God Blessing" me as if she was the Pope and my soul was at risk because I lived in a secular world. Her holiness got old fast.

About two months passed. When I got home from my job at the Telephone Company, Frannie called. She was home. The Mistress of Novices had told her to go home and reflect on her vocation. It seems the boss-nun suspected Frannie did not have a calling. Frannie was crushed. I was delighted.

"It wasn't just the Mistress, it was also her Roliness, the big fat Mother Superior. The moment she laid eyes on me, I knew she disliked me. Maybe because of my mother's divorce. Who is she to say God doesn't want me in His service? I'm going back," spewed my determined nun friend with the well-scrubbed face.

Frannie was insufferably subdued and pious for about six weeks. She lectured me because I didn't attend daily mass. Even suggested I join the Third Order of St. Francis, as she was going to do. This would permit me to be buried in the brown cassock of the Order.

"Brown is not my color," I responded, looking at her as if she was nuts.

Gradually, she confessed. Convent life was unbearable. "I hated the Latin, *Vidi aquam, ut supra.* Who cares?" she waved her hands mid air. "And after school you're nothing but a servant working in unbearable Florida humidity. Cooking, washing dishes, and ugh those depressing clothes," she said. "I had the other postulants in hysterics as I danced the can-can and the Mistress of Novices caught me. Then just once, I asked the kid who lived next door to the convent to turn up his radio. Benny Goodman was playing 'Frenasi'. Her Roliness heard me ask him and went bonkers. For the love of Pete, we were outside. It was during recess."

Soon the Max Factor Tan No. 2 was evident. The blonde streaks were back in her hair. Tangee lip-stick contoured her lips. Platform-soled high-heeled pumps that made her appear taller were pulled out of the closet. She asked me to call her Fran, not Frannie. She now went to the Raymor/ Playmor ballrooms with her kid sister. I had outgrown that gig. The war was on by now. I went to dances at the U.S.O. We did go to the Ken Club to dig jazz together on Sunday afternoons but it wasn't the same. All the cool cats were in the service. Then I went to Washington to work for the government.

Not long after I took the job in Washington, I came home to be her Maid of Honor. At nineteen, she married a clean-cut sailor named Phil, a good Catholic boy from Elizabeth, New Jersey whose favorite band was Guy Lombardo.

We have never lived in the same state again, but when we get together, old threads are picked up. Our conversations have more depth now. We no longer believe as children, but we both believe the role the Church played in our lives was significant. It has done us more good than harm. We decided her convent episode was either to atone for her parents' divorce or middle-child seeking attention.

Two silly, but morally sound young women, grew up and raised two good children in two good marriages. Today, our children think of us as squares. Fran became a lay-teacher in a Catholic school. I went to college at the expense of my corporate employer but never got a degree. Never taught, but have published poetry and prose. We have each overcome a lion's share of setbacks.

Fran looks like Angela Lansbury. I still don't look like Lauren Bacall, but when we meet after a long separation, the first one says. "I look so old, I've gained so much weight." On cue, the other says,

"That's not true. You look simply marvelous."

You can see, we are still funny.

Just Another Sunday

Overcast and raw, this Sunday began with a minor family conflict. Afraid it would rain, I decided I wouldn't wear my brand-new camel's hair coat to Sunday Mass.

"You said you bought a coat of quality. Surely the rain won't hurt it," my mother said. "We should always show new clothes to God first." I resented her insistence. I reminded her I had bought and paid for the coat with my own money, earnings from my first job. But I was only sixteen and my mother's influence on religious matters was strong. Now I feared if I didn't wear the coat, I wouldn't have any luck when I did.

At the kitchen mirror adjusting his tie my older brother Frank spoke up.

"Ma, who's God, some kinda fashion critic? Besides, it's God's day off. You're the one who said He rests on Sunday."

"Don't be blasphemous. It's to show God we're grateful for the work he provides so we can earn the money to buy clothes."

"Well the good Lord didn't find work for me," Frank said, shaking his head like a smart Alec over coffee. "That's why I had to join the Army."

"You couldn't lift that coffee mug if weren't for the Lord." My mother wagged her finger at my argumentative brother.

Patrick, the youngest, had gone to early Mass with my mother. Harry, a brother older than Frank, had gone with his girlfriend. The married members of my family took care of their own souls, but in my mother's house everyone except my father went to Mass. I think with him it was a case of male stubbornness.

"Hurry up or you'll be late," she shooed Frank and me out the door. I thought him splendid in his Private First Class uniform, but didn't say so. I also thought myself splendid. Though no one said so. I hoped heads would turn when I walked into the 11:30 a.m. Mass at Saint Benedict's Church. How could they miss me in my double-breasted camel's hair coat, so smartly accessorized with a brown cloche hat, leather gloves and almost new penny loafers.

Outside our house, we separated. Frank walked with his friends, and I hustled to pick up my friend, Frannie, outside the three family house where she lived.

"You look snazzy," she said. "It's the best coat I've ever seen on you."

"That's cause all the others were hand me downs from my sisters or cousins and most of the time they didn't fit," I said, grateful for Frannie's friendship.

After Mass, my mother had prepared the usual large Sunday dinner, and, as usual, no one was hungry. Frank and I, having just finished breakfast before Mass, picked at our food.

"If you fasted to receive Holy Communion you'd be hungry now," she scolded. In those days, the church ruled no food or drink after midnight until you received the Blessed Sacrament in the morning.

Since I hardly ate, I resented that I always had to wash the Sunday dinner dishes.

"I know you're a working girl now," my mother said, "'Nsure your buying your own clothes, but you're not paying us board." How could I on my part time income from Woolworth's Five and Dime?

My good-natured father sat at the kitchen table smoking and drinking his after-dinner tea. I was trying to enlist his help so I could make it to the 2:00 p.m. double feature at the Broadway Theater with Frannie. My mother sat at the dining room table reading the Sunday Globe. Home from the National Guard on a weekend pass, Frank played "Deep Purple" on the upright piano in the living room. I offered to buy him a pack of Camels to do the dishes, but no luck.

"Are you kidding? I had enough KP in basic training to last me a lifetime," he said.

That was it. Frank and Harry paid board, Patrick was too young. The only daughter still at home, I got stuck with washing dishes. But I was still working on my father.

As I stood at the gray stone sink washing dishes, or "had the privilege of diving for pearls" as my father joked, I heard footsteps on the back stairs of our second floor flat. Still whining about my Cinderella status, I heard a knock on the back door and a familiar voice.

"Frank, Frank. Open the door. Ith's Joe Ryan." Joe Ryan had a funny way of talking, I guess his tongue got stuck on the roof of his mouth when he said an "s".

"I wonder what news Biddie has today," I whispered to my father, and since he didn't get up, I wiped my hands on a towel and opened the back door. "Biddie" is what the Irish call a gossipy woman.

Joe was the sickly and only child of a woman almost too old to have children. His characteristics told you he lived in a fatherless home. His mother and aunt spent most of their day peering behind the curtains of their front bay window. You could feel their eyes on your back as they watched the comings and goings of everyone on the street. If I wanted to know anything, even about trouble in the making, I'd pump Joe. Not my favorite guy, since he told my brother, who told my mother, that I hung out with boys who gathered on the corner of our street. The result was I got, what I then considered, a deserved scolding for my indiscretion. "Wild" was the word they used to describe young girls who liked boys. I always felt obliged to tell the priest I had bad thoughts when I thought a boy cute.

I used Joe only as a valid gossip source. All the kids on the street would say, "Ask the Biddie, he'll know." In those days, feminine characteristics attributed to a man were the height of disrespect.

When I opened the door, I almost laughed out loud. Joe looked incongruous in a long wool overcoat and a soft gray fedora. His glasses low on his nose, his coat collar up around his neck, he looked like an actor in a Daschiel Hammett script.

"Wherths Frank? Isth he home?" he asked breathlessly, as if he had come on official business. "Isth important." Most neighborhood kids avoided Joe, but Frank was kind, one of the few kids on the street who tolerated Joe's company. So Joe considered him a friend.

"He's not stupid," Frank had defended Joe to the others guys. "His life is so empty, he has to invent conversation."

"Hasth he heard?" Joe's tobacco-stained fingers were shaking as he spoke. His face was whiter than usual. He removed his hat before he entered the house.

"Heard what?" I asked.

Joe hadn't worked a day since he got out of high school, two years before Frank did, but he always had cigarettes. In those days, no one but the Baptists recognized that smoking was unhealthy, but we kids knew smoking was bad for Joe.

"The Japenethe bombed Pearl Harbor early this morning."

"They did," I said as if I had heard of Pearl Harbor.

"Frank," I yelled over my shoulder, "Joe Ryan is here." Frank was finishing his song with a flourish. My mind supplied the lyrics, "You wander back to me, here in my Deep Purple dream." He never played a song the same way twice.

"Where's Pearl Harbor?" I was back at the sink, my hands in dishwater again.

"In Hawaii," my fathered answered, hopping out of his chair. He stood in the doorway that led to the dining and living rooms and shouted, "Frank, did you hear your sister? Joe Ryan is here to see you." His face was shaded with annoyance and alarm.

"Ith an important naval bayth in Hawaii," Joe answered my question again.

"Turn on the radio, Maggie," my father spoke to my mother who lifted her eyes from her newspaper and peered above her steel-rimmed bifocals to read my father's face. Without questioning, she got up and did as he asked

"The radio thez Roosevelt ith going to declare war on Japan," Joe said. By now my father was in the dining room fiddling with the Philco dial.

Frank walked past him, came into the kitchen smiling — until Joe told him what he had told us. Frank's expression changed.

Eyes popping behind his thick glasses, Joe continued, "They bombed the crap out of our naval base." He was anxious to blurt the news before the radio. "They demolished the Arizona. They're still counting the casualties."

"That's serious business," Frank said, now turning toward the radio in the dining room. "Roosevelt will have to declare war." His brow knitted. "We've heard rumors about helping England stop that guy Hitler. But nothing about the Japanese. I can't believe it! We can't let them get away with this!" Frank ranted and paced the dining room floor as my father turned the knob.

Now Gabriel Heater reported the news in grave tones. Everyone moved closer to the Philco.

"Mother of God," my mother said. "I remember the last war. So many American men were killed." She shook her finger in Frank's face. "I told you not to enlist." Her fears could rapidly turn to anger.

"Don't worry, Maggie," my father said, putting his arm around her shoulder. "Compared to the United States, Japan is the size of a postage stamp. We'll wipe them out in no time." He snapped his fingers to indicate speed.

"Are you sure, Jack?" She looked at him earnestly. She knew he read all the news, but mostly, she believed him because she wanted to. Now she reached over and patted Frank on his forearm almost apologetically.

I also believed my father. Later that day I sat in the movies with my friend Frannie just as I had on previous Sunday afternoons. I hadn't worn my new coat — too afraid of the rain that never came — too afraid I might get Hershey chocolate on it — not at all afraid because of what had happened at Pearl Harbor.

On Sunday nights previously, my parents tilted their heads toward the Philco and laughed, listening to the likes of Joe Penner, Jack Benny, or Fibber McGee and Molly. But on that night, radio time was consumed by news about Pearl Harbor casualties. A few days later, President Roosevelt addressed the Congress in that famous "This Day will be held in infamy" speech and asked for permission to declare war. Selfishly, it wasn't until I knew people killed in action that my innocence disappeared. Then, I became fearful.

Soon, Patrick and I were the only children living at home. We both attended early Mass with my mother. We had people to pray for. John, a brother who had moved away from home at nineteen, called to tell us not to worry. The fact that he did worried my mother. He had enlisted in the Merchant Marines. Harry soon enlisted in the Army Air Corps as a cadet, and Frank by now had transferred from the infantry to the paratroopers. My father, who never bought my mother's version of religion, now secretly went to Mass at 6:00 a.m. before he got home from his night job. A neighbor caught him and told my mother. My mother was wise enough not to mention she knew.

The next four years would seem like twenty. The war seemed endless. Three blue stars on a small, rayon-silk panel hung in our living room window. All three brothers were on foreign soil. Ration coupons, blackouts and A.P.O. addresses became the norm. Americans lost their loved ones, but we suffered and sacrificed little compared to the rest of the world. We knew about the bombings, but it wasn't until after the war that we heard what Hitler had done to European Jews. We felt ashamed that we dared to complain about our loss and deprivation.

Joe Ryan, by now the street's Air Raid Warden, had been classified as 4-F due to a congenital heart condition we never knew he had. We called him our Ernie Pyle after a great war correspondent of that era. Joe's gossip was now war news. I, for one, no longer called him Biddie. He gave support to neighbors when the messenger from the War Department delivered a black edged telegram. I guess his mother and aunt were still at their window. Now, he joined us often for Sunday dinner and wrote to Frank faithfully. After dinner, he traced movements of American troops across Europe and Asia on maps spread out on our dining room table. Something about knowing made us feel in control. Joe became a concerned friend of the family who taught me to look beyond the person you think you know. I regretted ever making fun of him.

War brings out the best and worst in people. Folks who formerly whined about and criticized America suddenly became nationalistic and patriotic. The lives of those we loved were at stake. The war effort was our focus. I left home in 1945 to work as an army civilian in Washington, D.C., too late to be of service. From there on V-J Day, I called my parents to rejoice. All my brothers had survived. Afterward, I went out and celebrated with all of Washington and an Ensign whose name I can't remember.

Sunday, December 7, 1941, was a day Americans of my generation will never forget. Those of us still living can tell you where we were and what we were doing when we heard the news. I use that incident to gauge my growth. A self-centered teenager, the Pearl Harbor attack was simply fodder for a newsreel I saw that accompanied a Sunday-afternoon double-feature movie. Bombs dropped on the other side of a continent didn't hit me, but soon they would shatter my life. The attack on Pearl Harbor changed my Sundays forever.

He Came in a Cup

All the Nolan women read tea leaves, but my mother's readings were the best. At least, that's what her sisters said.

"That's not true," my mother said when I quoted my aunts, Nora and Kitty. "Mary is the best, but she lives too far. I'm handy, that's all." My mother gave few compliments so she never accepted them.

How often I think of the three sisters, Maggie, Nora and Kitty, sitting around the oil-cloth covered kitchen table in that second floor flat on Crescent Street sipping tea from prized Irish Beleek cups. Low afternoon winter sun filtered through those awful bright yellow curtains my sister Margaret made to cheer the gray linoleumed kitchen. The curtains failed their mission. Their brassy color and organdy newness made the rest of the kitchen more drab. It was like a woman wearing a velvet, veiled-hat with flannel pajamas.

"I told you to buy the curtains we saw at Grant's," says Kitty, the tactless sister, "These look like mustard."

"Maybe goldenrod," Aunt Nora says, "Don't worry

Mag. They'll fade in the wash."

"Don't say a word against them to my Margaret. She spent hours making them," my mother says.

Bound at birth by blood and bound in friendship by adversity, the sisters got together about once a week. After the wash or housework was done, they would change house dresses to rayon prints, put on warm coats and hats and walk to each other's houses for a welcome cup of brewed hot tea. They lived in the same town in proximity to one another. Nora, who lived the farthest, walked a mile, picking up Kitty on the last half. Good thing. Kitty was the only sister too vain to wear orthopedic shoes. It was a long walk by today's standard, but in the 1930s walking was a common mode of travel. If husbands owned cars, they took them to work. It didn't matter, even if they had access to a car, my aunts and my mother, never dreamed of learning to drive. It was almost unfeminine. They considered themselves fortunate to have telephones because when the bills got behind, the telephone was the first thing to go. Then they got messages from each other by inconveniencing a good-natured neighbor.

When I came home from school famished, to a kitchen filled with the aroma of tea and homemade bread, the sisters made room at the table so I could have a cup of cocoa and a slab of my mother's first-rate bread with butter or jam. My brothers had eaten and left to play, but I stayed. If the gossip got too juicy, my mother's bent thumb in the direction of the door told me to leave the room. "Little pitchers have big ears," she'd say to her sisters.

When allowed to stay at the table, I savored the sisters' every word. I had often asked my mother to read my tea leaves, but she said neither the tea nor the readings were good for me. The Church didn't approve. We were putting false gods before God. It was okay for them, the adults, because they didn't take it seriously. This confused me, but my mother often used double talk to justify her actions. Like playing the numbers wasn't gambling because they knew they wouldn't win. I knew my mother and aunts' took the tea leaf reading seriously because often I overheard my mother on the phone talking to one of my aunts,

"See now, didn't I tell you that you were going to get a letter that would bring good news?"

Now, back at our kitchen, Maggie, my mother, says, "Kitty if you want me to read your fortune twist the cup around again. You only turned it twice." The cup had to be twisted upside down.

"Mary only does it twice," says Aunt Kitty. "As if it's going to make a big difference in the outcome."

"I don't care what sister Mary does, I do readings my way. The way Ma taught me. The way they do it in Ireland."

"Well, for God's sake, we all had the same mother, didn't we?" Kitty says, haughtily.

"Do you want Maggie to read your tea leaves, or don't you?" my Aunt Nora says. "Mary is always cutting corners. She's such a slob. Maggie and I visited her last week, and you couldn't find a seat in the parlor there were so many clothes and stuff scattered around."

"God knows, I couldn't keep up with nine kids. I've only got one and I'm always cleaning." says Kitty, as she cups her long fingers over the china cup and twists it fully around, scraping my mother's Beleek saucer. I couldn't help think how well her red polished nails and soft hands set off her diamond ring and wedding band.

I saw my mother's eyes scan the room, nervously. She was no great shakes as a housekeeper herself. She screamed at us kids to tidy up mornings on days the sisters were coming.

It wasn't until I met Aunt Mary that I understood. Every Wednesday, my mother and Aunt Nora took the Boston Elevated across town to Roxbury to make the novena at the Mission Church. Then they visited their so-called sloppy sister who lived nearby. Mary was the oldest.

One Wednesday on my birthday my mother took me to the Mission Church for a treat.

"This is more than a regular church, it's called a Basilica," my mother explained. In the corner by the side altar, crutches were stacked from floor to ceiling.

"Those crutches once belonged to people who made a novena to Our Lady of Perpetual Help and they left them here when they were cured."

I was awestruck. I wondered if the Our Lady What's Her Name could cure the warts on the back of my hands. If she did, I vowed I would come back and make a novena to her when I could travel alone on the El. Then my mother took me across the street to a religious store. "I'll buy you something for your birthday." She almost bought me picture of the Sacred Heart of Jesus for my room. I never dared to tell her or the nuns that the bloody heart of Jesus terrified me. Thank God, it cost too much. Instead, she bought me a sterling-silver chain and medal embossed with Our Lady of Perpetual Help. I was thrilled. I wore the medal every day and prayed to Our Lady every Wednesday. In less than six months, my warts had all disappeared.

When we left the religious store, she took me to visit Aunt Mary. It was the first time I saw my aunt. It was summer, and when we came down the street to her house, she was sitting on her front porch drinking tea and eating jelly doughnuts for lunch.

"Have one," she said, handing me the cardboard box before we even sat down.

I liked her right away, but she was the fattest woman I had ever seen. No wonder she never visited us. Years later, when I saw a statue of Buddha I thought of Aunt Mary. She had lived up to her reputation of being funny and good-natured. Traits I expected from overweight people from then on. She won my favor not by doughnuts alone, but by two silver quarters she gave when she learned it was my birthday.

Now my mother squints, peering into Aunt Kitty's cup, "I see a man." Pause. "He's carrying something." Pause. "It looks like a bag." Longer pause. Then her expression is quizzical. "Are you expecting a visitor, Kit?"

"Not that I know of. What else do you see?"

"I see money scattered everywhere. Lots of money coming your way."

Aunt Kitty rubs her Joan Crawford hands, saying, "I could use some."

Aunt Nora looks at her with annoyance. I know why. Aunt Kitty is the stingiest of the my mother's three sisters. She has only one child, her husband works steady as a night watchman. She and her daughter dress up-to-the-minute, but she never gave us kids a nickel. She whines constantly about money.

I stand behind my mother, look over her shoulder, and ask questions.

"Where is the man? Where is the money? All I can see is wet tea leaves."

My mother takes her pinky, points out a leaf shaped with a head, torso and what might be legs. I squint too. Eventually, I can see him. My mother's hands are rough, her lonely wedding ring is buried in red flesh.

"Where's the bag?"

"See, there, right next to him." She points out a square tealeaf. I had been thinking a sack over his shoulder.

"Can't you see all the money scattered above his head?"

"All I can see is little grains of tea."

"That's always a sign of money," Aunt Nora nods affirmatively to confirm my mother's position.

"Yes, yes, what else do you see?" says Kitty anxiously.

"I also see tears. Maybe the visitor is not such good news," my mother says.

"I know who it is." Aunt Nora slaps the table in a four-quarter beat. "Of course, of course. It's cousin Liam. The one in Ireland who just lost his wife. He wrote brother Pat, to say he's coming to Boston. He's looking for a place to stay until he gets settled."

"I hope he doesn't think he'll be staying with me!" Aunt Kitty rears her head. "My Bill doesn't like me to have company overnight." She gives my mother a dirty look as if it's her fault Liam is coming.

"Well, Mag, does he have any money in the bag?"

"For God's sake, Kit, I don't know who the man is, what he's got or where he's going. All I know is what I read in the tea leaves." In disgust, my mother turns her attention to Nora.

"Now, Nora, twist your cup three times."

With slight variations, Aunt Nora receives the same reading every week. My mother could always see Nora's four sons surrounded by lots of money, or she'd be going on a trip over water where people greeted her with warm and opened arms. Every trip in the cup would be the Ireland they never got back to in their lifetime. But a trip to Revere or Nantasket Beach nearby, where they ran into a neighbor or friend could fulfill the tea cup reader's prophecy.

Then it came time for Aunt Nora to read my mother's cup.

"I see a tall thin man coming towards you. It can't

be cousin Liam. He's too fat. Do you know this tall thin man, Mag? He's not your Jack."

"No," my mother says, "But put butter on his head and throw him under the table." And they did just that — they dipped the tealeaf in the butter dish and threw it under the table.

"Why do you do that?" I ask, knowing I'd be scolded if I did such a thing.

"So he won't become a foe," my mother says, as if it makes perfect sense, and goes right back to the reading.

Somehow Nora always found good fortune in my mother's cup. I was the small leaf, next to my sister, Margaret, the big leaf. And the leaf across the cup from us was my married sister, Marguerite. Aunt Nora, God Bless her, always gave me a promising future.

Later, in my early twenties, I did go back to the Mission Church on nine Wednesday nights to make my own novena to Our Lady of Perpetual Help — who, now that I think of it, answered my prayers once more. Our Lady found me the good husband I prayed for — and just maybe, he was the tall thin guy Aunt Nora saw in the teacup. I'm so glad the sisters took the time to butter his head.

The Kitchen Table

Details of the kitchen table we had in that row house in Charlestown elude me, but how well I remember all the tables after that first one.

I was only five when my parents decided to move us to a large four-bedroom house in then rural Revere. The kitchen table in that second house was huge with thick, turned bulbous legs. Oak or walnut, I'd say. Six chairs matched, four were mongrels. Ten of us could eat at one sitting. The long table sat between two west windows. It jutted out into the middle of the big kitchen that overlooked our huge back yard, garage and driveway.

Who cares about kitchen tables? Well, I do. I mourn the loss of kitchen tables. Something was lost when they were replaced with kitchen counters. In my day, counters were for restaurants, drugstores, and for sales clerks to stand behind. Maybe those thick Formica™ slabs saved space and are more efficient, but do they replace a table? I don't think so.

Lives were shaped at kitchen tables. Opinions were voiced, arguments settled and parental justice was administered as we sat there.

At the Revere kitchen table, my mother and nineteen-year-old brother John not only started a business, they ended it there.

"We're not making any profit selling our doughnuts," my mother said, handing John a list of figures to read as we sat around after supper. "We'll have to quit the doughnut business." She made them: John sold them. They had worked hard at it for four months.

"You can't do that." I protested, "I love those doughnuts."

"This doesn't concern you," my father said.

John whipped the pages from my mother's hand and scanned them.

"This can't be true. Your figures must be wrong." John's heart was in that business. I thought he would cry. Maybe he did cry. I was sent from the room when a big argument began. I learned later John had called my mother stupid and my father almost hit him. Shortly after that argument, John ran away from home. So, John wasn't with us when we moved to Somerville, but the huge kitchen table moved with us.

I recall sitting around it one night at supper as the smell of hamburger and onions frying pleases me. I love the anticipated meal: mashed potatoes drenched with hamburg and onion gravy. My mother spoons out mashed potatoes to each child at the table. She stops behind me. As she spoons my share on to my plate, she says,

"Was it you Mrs. Ryan said she saw talking to the boys on the corner? I told you nice girls don't hang out on street corners with the boys. If hear about it again, you'll be punished."

"She embarrasses me. I tell her to go home," my big-mouthed brother Harry said.

"And who's talking to you, Big Shot?" my mother said, putting him in his place. It's something she didn't do often enough to suit me. I learned early that boys' rules did not apply to girls, and boys as a result had more fun.

Our kitchen was the family room. The coal furnace wasn't fired up until late November, so we gathered in the only heated room. That big kitchen in that Somerville flat was like a library in a mansion. We knitted, colored, read, did homework, and would you believe, we prayed around it. We knew the day by smell: Sunday, spare ribs; Monday, hamburger; Tuesday, spaghetti; Wednesday, mutton stew; Thursday, hash; Friday, fish or corn chowder; and Saturday, baked beans and bread. If the radio wasn't on the table, it was close by. Its only competition was a book or an argument.

Money was scarce then, but for a nickel or less, my mother bought outdated magazines or old books to entertain us.

"Ma's got books from Sally's," I'd yell to Patrick and Frank when I saw her walking up the street from the bus stop toting her leatherette book bag. Sally's was what we called the Salvation Army Store in Boston. We didn't want certain lace-curtain Irish neighbors to know she shopped second hand.

The bag would bulge with *Popular Mechanics*, Dick Tracy comic books for my brothers and fashion or storybooks for my sisters and me. She'd empty everything on the kitchen table and we'd fight for first dibs pushing and shoving like cedar waxwings at a bush of berries.

After supper on those winter evenings, we'd sip cocoa or tea while we read. Frank would go nuts because my sister Margaret made noise eating peanut butter and crackers. I hadn't even noticed. What bothered me is that she hogged two chairs, one to sit on and one for her feet. The rest of us didn't have that privilege but she was the oldest at home.

"Aha," Frank said with pride one night. "I hid the Saltines. We won't have to listen to her tonight."

Margaret spent fifteen minutes looking for the crackers and when she couldn't find them, she opened the refrigerator and took out celery. Now the crunching really began.

When we moved to yet another house in Somerville, we had to dump that big kitchen table. It wouldn't fit. We bought a small, round, maple table. By now my sisters were married and three of my brothers were in the armed forces. It suited four of us still at home.

At all our kitchen tables we played cards, or Beano,

as Bingo was called in those days. It was where my mother and her sisters read fortunes using tealeaves or cards to foretell a future of promise. What's nice about any kitchen table is that you could look across and read each other's expression. You could determine if the fortune teller was disclosing everything, if your brother held the ace, or if your parents meant it when they warned, "No more fighting or you'll all go to bed."

A close friend would be invited to eat at your kitchen table. It was cozier than the dining room table, which was used for holidays or company and was always covered with a fancy tablecloth. You didn't have to be on your best behavior with oilcloth. Spills wiped up easily. You could get away with reaching to get what you needed if someone didn't respond to your request.

When family finances improved, sometime in the mid 40s, we moved to Everett and gave away that kitchen table and replaced it with a modern, art deco type with a metal enameled top. Each of its six maple chairs weighed as much as the table. The top was beige, overlaid with a brown swirled design. You could make it larger by lifting the leaves or smaller by unhinging them. Every dish you set on it clanged. I never liked it. But my mother said it was the latest style and it suited her needs. The family size dwindled as we all pursued our own lifestyles, some of us buying our own kitchen tables.

After I married, all my kitchen tables were wooden. We managed to squeeze a small antique table into our smallest, most recent kitchen. When my children left home, my husband convinced me that for practical purposes, we should replace it with a counter. We did, and we never use the counter except to put the groceries down before we put them away or to clutter it with incoming mail. The two of us eat at the long, pine table in what is called the dining area. The table is too big, but it's useful when the children and grandchildren come for dinner.

As I wrote this piece I learned that maybe it wasn't the kitchen table I missed, but the intimacy I shared with the people around it: first my parents and my brothers and sisters, and then my husband and children. It doesn't matter whether we fought or exchanged pleasantries with one another: the family defines who we are or who we become either because, or in spite, of them.

What I really feel is that the people around my kitchen tables outgrew their seats too soon.

I Hardly Knew John

On a warm May day, my impulsive brother John put my three-year-old brother, Patrick, in a stroller and pushed him all the way from our house in Revere, through Malden, through Everett, to Sullivan Square up Bunker Hill Street, down Allston Street to visit my Aunt Nora in Charlestown. I'd say it was an eight or ten-mile push.

Home from shopping at about 3 p.m., my mother found a note on the kitchen table. "Took Patrick for a walk. Love, John."

"They ought to be along any minute," she told me when I came from school at four and wanted to play with baby Patrick.

She fretted two and half-hours. The phone rang and I heard her yell, "What do you mean you've got blisters on your heels?" She turned to my father. "It's your crazy son John. He's at my sister Nora's. He walked all the way and now he wants you to come get him."

My father grabbed the tall black phone. "I'll give

you blisters on your head when you get home. You walked there: walk home," my father said, hanging up the phone with force.

"You'll have to drive over to Nora's and get him."

"Tell him to borrow a dime from Nora and take the El."

"He can't. He's got Patrick and the stroller with him."

"Jesus H. Christ!" my father shouted putting down his fork. I didn't know where the "H" came from in Christ's name, but it meant my father was really angry. Maybe it was added so the real Christ wasn't blasphemed. "That boy's got oatmeal for brains." He pushed back his chair, and left his unfinished supper. I bet John caught hell on the ride home but nothing phased him.

John was always in trouble. One Sunday after dinner, his turn to wash pots and pans, he threw my mother's big roasting pan in the tall grass so he wouldn't have to wash it. My mother searched for weeks, until the day my father let a neighbor scythe our backfield to use for hay. When my father appeared at the back door, dirty pan in hand, my mother knew. "Johneee," she shrieked so loud Patrick ran and hid under the bed.

A few years later, it was the same impulsive and innovative John who put my mother into the doughnut business. My father had lost the best job he ever had as Traffic Manager of a large sand and gravel company,

We were living in that huge house in Revere. The house had a big back yard, lovely parquet floors and French doors. It also had a cellar kitchen with two soapstone sinks and a four-burner gas stove. All our Italian neighbors had two kitchens — one cool and dark for summer in the basement, and one sunny and bright upstairs in winter. The house had been built for an Italian merchant who never moved in. My father bought it from the bank.

Mondays, my mother did laundry in the basement. My father brewed beer and root beer there. My brother Frank tinkered with engines, and I chalked and played hopscotch on its cement floor — but we never used it as a kitchen until John had a scheme to keep the family afloat.

"I'll drum up the customers, Ma, and you make the doughnuts. We've got the perfect cellar."

"Don't be foolish. Who'd buy my doughnuts?"

"Ma, we're going to lose this house if we don't come up with the mortgage. Pa hasn't worked in months and you haven't got Marguerite's board to count on now." This sister had recently married. John's first task of salesmanship was selling my mother. "Everybody loves your doughnuts. Of course they'd buy them." He succeeded in selling her.

Before we knew it, my unemployed father was sawing lumber to build a long utility table at which she could roll dough and cut her doughnuts. On Saturdays, she let me help. I loved plunging the cutter into the soft mass to create a circular work of art. Though my mother wouldn't let me drop them into the kettles, I was fascinated how the hot fat puffed my limp creations into real live doughnuts. I considered it my talent. Sugaring was another assignment. After I rolled them in the sweet crystals, I'd lick my succulent fingers. That and my salary of three or four donut holes made my mother and brother's enterprise a pleasant experience for me.

My mother bragged to Aunt Nora about John. "He could sell a woman in Florida a raccoon coat."

"Let me talk to Johnnie," the customers would say when they telephoned to order. He'd come to the phone, pencil in his ear, and call them by first names. I was so impressed.

The smell of doughnuts frying rose up into the bedrooms of the house, and when the rest of us awoke the house was warm. Poor John and my mother had been up since 4:30 a.m. to prepare orders. Dozens of doughnuts had been cooked, drained, and packed into wax paper bags. Snow, cold or ice in winter — nothing deterred John. In mackinaw and galoshes he drove my father's car, tire chains flapping on snowy roads, to service customers. John's success puffed him with pride.

On the brink of manhood at nineteen, John was a charmer. Dark, wavy hair, he pushed curls off the forehead that hung over thick-lashed blue eyes. A back slapper, he'd treat people as if he had known them before they were born. Women loved him. "A shameless flirt," my mother said. Not tall, but he was broad shouldered and massive looking. He had worked intensively to establish the routes he serviced. He had reason to be proud.

It soon became difficult to keep up with his success. They had restaurants and grocery stores after their product. Too many orders for a two-person operation with only one car. My father tried to help but he only he got in my mother's way. When John returned from his morning route, my father needed the car to look for a job or work per diem as a mechanic or laborer. Afternoons, John and my mother sat at a second hand kitchen table, counted money, made lists of supplies and route schedules. They worked efficiently, but something was wrong.

At first my mother used the materials she had on hand, so the profits were large. As time went on, she figured "In money" and "Out money," as she called her debits and credits, and found she wasn't making a profit.

"We're big Johnnie, but not quite big enough to hire someone else to keep up with the orders," my mother said, "I'm barely able to pay you, and you work so bloody hard." John, a social animal, needed the twelve dollars a week she paid him. They got a wholesaler to sell them supplies, but they never ordered enough to get bulk discounts.

Six months into the business, my father, mother and John sat around the upstairs kitchen table drinking coffee and eating doughnuts. John's face sobered when, with pen and ink, my mother proved they were losing money.

"I'll get more customers," John pleaded. According to Frank they had a big argument.

"John, no one wants doughnuts for lunch. You just about make the routes by nine thirty as it is," my father said.

"If we buy another car, you can drive a route." John said.

"We don't have the money for another car," my mother said, "We can barely keep this one in repair and gasoline. Your father makes more money doing odd jobs for garages."

About then, John called my parents ignorant.

"As long as you live in this house, you'll treat us with respect," my father shouted. It was shortly after this that John ran away from home. I say run away. Not exactly. He was old enough to be on his own. He just left. Without a why or goodbye. I don't know when he left, or what he took with him. We weren't told, but I knew something was amiss when my mother was at the stove crying and my father hugged her.

"It's not your fault, Maggie."

I thought someone had died she was so sad. Days passed before I missed John, as he was never around mornings when I left for school. When I came home, John was asleep. I always went out to play and never came in until supper.

"Johnnie's run away from home," my brother Frank said. I had visions of John running down the street away from our house with kerchief and stick over his shoulder like the boy on the Horatio Alger book cover.

"Where did Johnnie run to?" I asked my mother.

She sighed deeply and said, "God only knows where he is. Say a prayer. Ask the Virgin Mary to watch over him."

A year or so later, after we moved from the house in Revere to Somerville, John appeared at our door with another man. My parents were so glad to see him, they didn't even yell. I think he brought the man so my parents would be polite. John had joined the Merchant Marines. If my father lectured him, it was not in front of the rest of us. It was pre-World War II days. John fascinated us with stories of carrying arms to Great Britain.

He wasn't a great correspondent, but after he made amends, he kept in touch. When the war broke out he wrote my mother to say he had married a woman from New Jersey and they had a son. My mother read me part of a letter he wrote — either I had achieved adult status or I was the only child left she could confide in. By now, everyone but Patrick and I had left home for war or marriage.

"Dear Ma and Pa,
I'm sorry for leaving like I did. Before I had a kid
of my own, I didn't know how much people care
about their kids. You must have been worried sick
about me. You treated me okay and I shouldn't
have left home like that. I blamed you cause the
doughnut thing didn't work out, but I know now
it was no ones fault."

She carried that letter with her for years. As if it was proof that she was a good parent and John's leaving was not her fault.

During the war John seemed to get home often enough to increase the size of his family. I know he had four children. I also heard from my father, who visited him in Hoboken, New Jersey after the war, that he was still crazy.

"He's got a good job as a bus driver," my father said. "He insisted I go on the route with him. He knew everyone who got on the bus by name and they knew him and all his kids. Seems he used to take them with him although it was against company rules to have free riders. The man has no respect for authority."

"The wife shouldn't let the kids go with him," my mother said.

"She's as irresponsible as he is. She left her ten-year old taking care of the kids while she went shopping. They're both wacky," my father said.

One of my teenage nephews went to visit John and got stuck taking care of his five children for the weekend. He agreed to baby-sit while they went out for the evening to dinner, but John and his wife took off for Atlantic City for the weekend from where John called to see if everything was all right. My sister Marguerite, my nephew's mother, was furious. She never allowed her children to visit John again.

John often drove to Massachusetts from New Jersey to visit us without announcement. Sometimes he brought a friend, one of his kids or all of them. Once, he tried to date one of my girlfriends Disgusted. I told my father who insisted John was only joking. But my father must have said something to John because he apologized to me, said he was just trying to make her feel good. I suspected John was a womanizer.

John divorced his first wife after several years of marriage. He claimed she was an alcoholic. I had always thought he was. Who knows? No one in our family really knew him after he left home at nineteen, and I hardly knew him before then. I suspect he was a drinker who went to work everyday so he didn't consider himself an alcoholic. I don't think he was abusive, but he was irresponsible.

"If John and his wife lived next door to me, I'd do my best to avoid them," I once said to my brother Harry. He was shocked by my attitude.

"He was great fun growing up," Harry said. He may have been, but I never saw that side of him. Out of my five brothers, I admired John the least, but I only remember the bad stuff. Maybe he straightened out as he matured.

When my sister Marguerite's youngest child, Michael, married, John came from New Jersey sporting a new wife. She spoke English well, but with a heavy accent.

"We've been married a year," she said. "I am a refugee. I met your brother at a dance at the Hungarian Club. He is so funny, your brother."

"Can you believe it? Me. Married to a classy lady like her?" John said. I had only met John's first wife once, but there was no comparing the two women. Julie was tiny and always looked tired.

Sophie, the new wife, was well dressed, dark skin

set off by lots of gold jewelry and wearing an under-stated beige and black two-piece dress. Though she appeared ten years younger than John, you could tell she thought her fifty-year-old husband was quite a catch. It was the way she looked at him when she straightened his tie and coat lapels.

John had a cavalier John Wayne persona with his curly dark hair, broad shoulders, and laughing Irish eyes. He seemed just tickled to be John and thought everyone else felt the same way. He wore a navy blazer and wool flannel pants, not the frumpy unmatched jacket and baggy pants he had worn on previous visits.

"Did you know I'm now a big shot," he told every-one at the bridal table. "I'm a supervisor for the bus company."

"Good for you," someone said.

"Yup, ever since I joined AA, my life has turned around. Look at my wife, isn't she something." He squeezed her hand on the table and she looked up at him smiling.

"I joined AA when I found out I was diabetic."

"How much insulin do you take?" our sister, Marguerite, asked. She was also a late onset diabetic.

"None, I stopped taking it."

"That's dangerous," Marguerite said. Then, there was a multi-family discussion around the bridal table on the subject of diabetes. It seemed John's new wife trusted nature more than doctors.

"My John is on a very healthy diet," his new wife

Sophie said. John held onto her every word. Sophie was a fine example of good health. She had thick hair, good skin, and strong white teeth.

"Insulin is a chemical and the body makes it own." Sophie lectured us now. "You Americans take too much medicine. If you eat good natural food, your body will be healthy, your insulin will balance itself in the pancreas." she said. "Look at him, does he look unhealthy. He eats good food — no sugar — lots of natural grain bread — lots of fresh fruit." I couldn't argue, I didn't know much about diabetes then, but I knew John never looked better. Rosy cheeks, skin glowing, and for once, his belly did not hang over his belt.

Though usually non-combative, Marguerite argued hotly with Sophie pointing out the danger of not taking insulin. Marguerite, our surrogate mother, was invested in all of us, but she and John had a special friendship growing up. She always made excuses for him to my parents. She finally gave up talking to Sophie. Her final statement was to John.

"Do what your doctor says or you're going to be in trouble. You're not a borderline diabetic you're a full-blooded one like me. Please, get back on the insulin right away."

"You know how I hate that needle," John said, wincing like a child.

A few years later, Sophie called my parents to say John had a cerebral hemorrhage and died.

The News About Arthur

Wearing cotton-knit bloomers and undershirt, I came downstairs, used the bathroom and came out shivering. I crossed the kitchen and held my small hands over the black, chrome-trimmed stove embossed with a name I had just learned to read: "McGee". It was Saturday. No school. October morning sun streamed through the window making hopscotch like squares of light on the gray-blue patterned linoleum. It wasn't a warm sun.

"Go back upstairs and get your bathrobe," my mother's voice came over my shoulders as she came out of the pantry. "You're getting too old to run around the house in your underwear." She was fully dressed and wore a sweater. "And find those slippers I bought you," she yelled up the staircase that led from the kitchen to the upstairs bedroom.

I didn't own pajamas. My older sisters said I should, not my mother.

"Growing up in Ireland, we all slept in our underwear and we turned out fine," she said.

When I came downstairs again, a man had taken my spot by the stove. He too, was warming his hands. His back to me, he wore dark woolen trousers and a sleeveless undershirt, suspenders hung on each side. Bandages were wrapped from under his left arm to his right shoulder.

I had heard the front door open during the night and my father's voice. I turned over, went right back to sleep thinking my father had to leave his bed to go pick up a driver whose truck had broken down. It happened often. I assumed he brought the driver home with him.

When I managed to face the man, I knew it wasn't a driver. It was Arthur. "Hello," I said to the brother I seldom saw. He was twenty-seven when I was six. I knew him as the brother who married a woman with marcelled, dark hair, deep-set brown eyes and skin as smooth as evaporated milk. Eleanor looked like a 1920's movie star. They had two little boys who never visited us. They lived in a place called Jamaica Plain, far away from our house in Revere. I went there once with my father to pick up a Persian rug for our dining room. His house was stylishly modern, neat as a pin, looked as if no one lived there. Junior the oldest boy was almost my age. Skinny, he sucked two fingers all the time. Danny was fat faced and robust. Just a little kid like my brother Pat. Much friend-lier than his brother Junior, or Juny, as we called him.

Patrick and I sat in the car when my father went inside, but soon Eleanor came out and told us to come in.

"Make yourself at home," she said. She gave us milk and cookies. We chuckled when she said, "Boys, meet your aunt and uncle."

Now in front of our kitchen stove, I stared at Arthur in disbelief until he looked down.

"Why it's little Rosie!" he said, "My but you've grown in two years time." He smiled the smile of a patronizing adult.

I wanted to ask what happened to his arm, but I hesitated. Didn't feel I knew him that well. I wondered why we never saw him. My sister Marguerite was married but I saw her lots.

"Arthur, what do you eat for breakfast?" I heard my mother ask. The coffee was already on the stove and the tin of evaporated milk and Wonder Bread™ set on the table. She held two white ironstone mugs in her hand.

"Coffee, toast, anything. I'm not hungry," he said, running his fingers through his thick kinky hair. His long thin face had a yellow tinge.

"Where are your little boys?" I asked.

"They're staying with Marguerite."

"Eat your cereal and stop asking so many questions. Arthur's had an accident. He doesn't feel like talking."

Arthur ruffled my head with his left hand as much as to say that's okay. When my father got up, the four of us sat at the table in silence and ate. One-by-one my brothers showed up for breakfast. All surprised to see Arthur.

"What the Hell happened to you?" said my brother John.

"I've had an accident. A gun went off accidentally and hit me."

"A gun," John said. "Where in Christ's name did you get a gun?"

John often used swear words. My mother scolded him about taking the Lord's name in vain, but John didn't listen unless my father got after him.

"I sell diamonds you know. My boss gave it to me."

I knew what diamonds were. Right away, I held my brother Arthur in esteem. No wonder he was so distant. He was rich.

Soon after breakfast Frank, Patrick and I, the three youngest, were ushered out. My father had a chicken coop in the backyard of that Revere house, and we were told to go gather the eggs and feed them. It was something my father usually supervised; this time he didn't. The older children, Margaret, Harry and John sat at the table with my father, mother and Arthur.

"I wonder why Junior and Danny aren't staying here?" I said, once we got outside.

"Yeah. And where's Eleanor? Something's fishy," my brother Frank said. "Imagine, someone in our family owns a gun. Wait till I tell Joe." Joe was his best friend in Revere. "It's just like the movies."

When we brought the eggs to the kitchen, my mother looked up from the discussion and decided she had another errand for us.

"Go over to Rubino's and get two loaves of fresh Italian bread," she said. Rubino's was the small grocery store we shopped in when we couldn't get to the distant A&P. "We'll have Italian spaghetti for supper," she added. She learned to make it from our Italian neighbors and we all loved it, but it was a company meal that took all day to cook. I figured Arthur's wife, Eleanor, was coming. No hot dogs and canned beans for company.

Before we left the house, Arthur gave us each a penny for candy.

"Tell, Mrs. Rubino if it's not fresh, it's going back," my mother said, acting like herself for the first time that day.

Patrick and I were standing at the glass cage that held the penny candy. When Frank shouted, "Holy Toledo, Rosie. Come here. Look at this."

There on the first page of the Daily Record, was a full-framed photograph of my brother Arthur holding a bleeding shoulder. Each finger of his hand and the front of his shirt was covered with black blood. In the background was his wife, Eleanor. She was wearing a black coat and her head was bent down. A fat cop held her by the arm. I thought she was sad because Arthur was hurt, but I was just old enough to sound out the headline above. "Woman Shoots Husband in Family Dispute."

"What's dis poo tee?" I asked.

"Dispute stupid. It's a fight, an argument," Frank said.

"Wow, " I said, "Our big brother is a celebrity."

Mrs. Rubino overheard us as she stood over our shoulders.

"Thatsa your brother, Frankie? I never sawd him before. Wow. Too bad for your mother and father." Frank and I decided to chip in our pennies to buy the paper. My family only read the Boston Globe. Little Patrick got penny candy.

We ran home, forgetting the bread. My mother threw up her hands when she saw the paper.

"Oh my God, now everyone will know."

Arthur's first comment was that it was a lousy picture of him.

Now that we were in on the truth, the situation was not discussed with us, but at least in front of us. Through snatches of conversation, I learned my brother and his wife were big party people — entertained a lot — seems as a result Eleanor drank something called highballs — too many. The shooting took place after a party and many highballs. The reason she was not with Arthur was because she was in jail. In jail! I repeated these words over and over to myself. His children were brought to my married sister Marguerite's house in the middle of the night. My father had picked up Arthur at the hospital where he had been treated and then brought him to our house.

The telephone rang all day. Reporters trying to get details. I stretched my little ears to hear gossip about Eleanor and Arthur.

Marguerite stopped by our house after lunch with Arthur's boys.

"I'm not surprised this happened," she said. "Arthur was a tease and a snot growing up. Sometimes John and I felt like shooting him." My mother reprimanded her for talking that way, and said it was because they had lived high off the hog and that drink will do you in every time. My father, I could tell, was saddened by it all. "The poor youngsters" he said, watching Danny and Junior playing in the yard. I thought I was in a movie.

I thrived on drama even then so when Mrs. Bellotti and Mrs. Mantini cornered me against the Bellottis' dimpled-cement-block garage and pumped me for details about the shooting, I exaggerated, or told them everything I knew. Heck, when did I ever get to be the center of attention? Not Frank. He kept his mouth shut.

The Saturday after the shooting, my father drove me to Marguerite's flat in Malden so I could play with Arthur's boys. Juny and I were playing checkers when I heard a car. I looked out the living room window to see Arthur had pulled up in his big black Buick.

"Arthur's here and Eleanor's with him," I yelled so my sister could hear me in the kitchen.

"I'll be damned, she's with him. How'd he pull that one off? Where'd he get the money for her bail?" Marguerite said to her husband. I guessed they expected Arthur was coming because Danny and Juny's clothes were all packed.

Both boys jumped up from the rug where we had been playing. When he saw his mother, Danny burst out crying, "Mommy, Mommy, I want my Mommy." Arthur came in, his thin face still pale and tense. Danny ran toward him screaming, "Where's Mommy? I want my Mommy."

"Mommy's waiting in the car. We're all going home now. Give Auntie Marg a big kiss and thank Uncle Vin." A silent Juny stood next to Danny. As usual he acted as if what was happening had nothing to do with him until Marguerite hugged him goodbye. He clung to her legs fiercely. Then he began to sob a gasping sob that shook his skinny body until he got to the car. Then Eleanor stepped out of the car, bent down and embraced each boy in an arm. She kissed their tears, then wiped them with her fingers. I couldn't hear what she said, but I somehow knew she was crying too.

"I pity those poor kids," Marguerite said. Her husband, Vin, shook his head as adults do when they think something's hopeless.

A year or so later, we were living in Somerville when we learned Eleanor walked out on Arthur and her children. He pulled up to my mother's house and dropped off Danny. Junior had been dropped off at his adoring Godmother's house, Eleanor's childless sister. Danny lived with us for about two years.

Danny was easy. Good natured, and adorable like most three-year-old children. I'm not sure he got the nurturing a child his age needed, but he was treated like the rest of us. We took turns sleeping with him because whoever got him, awoke angrily, with a very wet back. He peed the bed every night and the victim always had to change him and the bed. Arthur came not every, but most, weekends. Perhaps Eleanor called my mother but she never came in person which bothered me because I loved looking at her.

"He'd take her back in a minute," Marguerite told my mother. "He's still crazy about her."

"Well he'd be crazy if he did. She drinks."

"Maybe it was Arthur's fault. Fancy clothes, big cars, and entertaining all those business swells and expected her to drink with them. I'd give him a good kick in the arse out the door. He never came to see us until he was in trouble. He offered me money for caring for his kids while she was in jail. He doesn't get it — everything's not about money."

It bothered me to hear Marguerite talk about the brother who wore a golden watch and cuff links with sharply creased pants and pointed-toe shoes. I thought him dashing. When he popped by to see Danny in his big car, he had compliments and pennies for all. Maybe his affection was insincere, but secretly, I was pleased someone in our family had been described in the newspaper as "well-heeled".

Eleanor never returned. One day Arthur and Juny picked up Danny, and they all moved to Kansas where Arthur sold advertising. He remarried twice. His third wife was a blonde, thin, wiry woman with a typical

Kansas accent, who seemed to adore him and was devoted to his sons. "The salt of the earth," my father said, after he visited them. "Arthur lucked out this time."

But his luck lasted only three years. Arthur was killed in a car accident at age thirty-nine.

"It's a tragedy that Daddy died so young," Juny told my father at the funeral, "But thank God it wasn't Mother. We'd be lost without her."

Marguerite's Heart

Crash! Splash! Startling sounds back-to-back awakened me from a deep sleep. Then — my mother's voice. Conversational. Couldn't make out her words. My father's response was equally hushed. I breathed a sigh of relief; at least my father wasn't in trouble. For a moment, I had thought maybe he'd gone up to Fushanti's again, drank homemade wine with the old man. That always made my mother yell. I turned over thinking it was Rover, our mongrel dog, who restlessly groaned and roamed the rooms of our huge Revere house at night.

The moon shining through the dormer window onto the double bed my big sisters shared showed me Margaret was there but Marguerite was missing. Something was very wrong.

"Didya hear that?" Margaret sat up and whispered.

"I heard somethin."

"Bet it was Marguerite sneaking in," she said, "She's going to get killed."

"Killed" meant punishment for minor offenses in our family not true homicide, but we knew our sister was in trouble. She had left the house earlier in the evening following an argument with my mother about the likes of the boy she was dating.

"He's nothing but an unpaid farmhand for his father," my mother said, clearing the supper dishes. "I left that life behind in Ireland. Who wants a life depending on the fickleness of crops while yer mucking around in pig sties? I want more for my daughters."

"She's eighteen. She'll get over him," my father said. They spoke as if Marguerite wasn't there.

"He's here every night in the week, hanging around like a dog in heat. She's got to be up at six, to work in Boston by eight."

As Marguerite left the house that night with Vinnie, the boy she called her sweetheart, my mother thumped her forefinger on the kitchen table. "You be in this house in bed by ten o'clock at the latest."

"Awright, awright," Marguerite said, throwing her white summer sweater over her shoulders. She wore nice clothes because she worked at Paramount Films' distribution center. Something to do with the winding of reels. She quit high school either to help the family financially or by choice to get the things she wanted.

The next day we learned what happened the night before. Marguerite, thirteen years my senior, got home late so my mother locked her out to force her to ring the bell announcing the time. The sweethearts tried to outsmart my mother. Vinnie jimmied open the cellar window, and pushed Marguerite's small body through. Trouble was, she either tripped over, or landed on, a barrel of my father's beer brewing in our basement.

My mother's conversation by then escalated to yelling.

"Is that you, Marguerite?" she shouted at the top of the cellar stairs. "Do you know what time it is? Vincent heard what I said when you went out the door? What kind of an omidon is he anyhow? I'll give him a piece of my mind if he ever comes around here again."

Vinnie's roadster crushed gravel on our driveway just as our darkened bedroom reeked of beer.

"Where is Ma now?" Margaret said, to the silhouetted figure of Marguerite that just appeared in our room.

"At the cellar stairs." Marguerite responded. "What am I going to do? I smell awful. I'm all sticky."

"I know one thing, you're not sleeping with me," Margaret said.

They decided Marguerite would sleep on my cot-sized bed and I would sleep with Margaret.

"Rosie, you go downstairs. Tell Mum she woke you with all her yelling and that you have to go to the bathroom. Then go into the bathroom. Stay there until she goes back to bed. Get me a face cloth, soap and a bowl of water. There's a bowl under the sink."

"I'm scared," I whined. But I knew Marguerite needed distance from my mother who was not quick to be physical, but as my father had said, her angry voice could break Waterford crystal at ten feet.

"Do it and I'll bring you home something nice on payday." Marguerite, whom we called Marg, did this anyhow. She was the kinder of my two older sisters.

The house smelled like a brewery for weeks, which increased the hostility between my mother and Vinnie, but it did not end the sweethearts' relationship. At first, Marg and Vin saw each other in secret, and eventually, openly. Vinnie was smart enough to keep a low profile. When my mother first saw him a month or so later, she was civil — but there was no "why don't you stay for supper" warmth.

I equated my sister's sweetheart, as she called him, with Tom Mix. Vinnie often stopped by to see my sister after his once-a-month National Guard Calvary weekend. He cut a romantic figure in his khaki, wide-brimmed softly dented hat, jodhpurs and riding boots. I dreamed some weekend he'd ride by on his horse and without stopping, scoop me under his arm and take me for a ride up the nearby Garabaldi's Hill.

Vinnie and Marg were two people I loved, and my mother hated one of them. She insisted they take me along on dates. You might think they would be unkind to me but they weren't. On Sunday afternoons they took me on walks or to a movie, even offered to pay to take me up in a plane once, but I was too afraid.

Every payday, Marguerite brought home a gift for my brothers and me. Stuff from the five and ten, but they could have been from Tiffany's for all they meant to us. I remember fat little Orphan Annie books, dime store pearls I cherished. She starched and ironed my school clothes because my mother hated to iron. Saturdays, she picked up the house because she couldn't stand chaos. She taught me how to make my twin bed because she said that's what big girls do. We three sisters shared the large front bedroom on the second floor of the house. Four of my brothers slept in one of equal size in the back.

Usually, I fell asleep before my sisters came to bed, but one night I overheard Marguerite tell Margaret that Vinnie wanted her to marry him. I didn't know it was a secret. All hell broke loose when I mentioned it to my mother who soon confronted Marguerite. When she didn't deny it, my mother yelled, "Over my dead body."

Even my father considered Marguerite too young. Vinnie's mother didn't approve either. Marguerite, a high school dropout, did not suit Nellie Mulligan's plan for a son who went to Boston College High and would go on to its college. Her son would do great things with his life — not work on a farm like his father, who as it turned out, was no slouch since he and his brother owned three commercial farms.

Vincent, his mother revealed, had been sent to Boston College in a car his parents supplied, but he never got there. Before he met Marguerite, he spent his days joy riding with friends. Working on the farm with his father was supposed to be punitive, but he seemed to prefer it to school.

Despite the opposition — Marg and Vin, as we called them, got married. She was nineteen. He was twenty-one. Ten months later they had their first child, then their second, then their third — Three children within four years on fifteen dollars a week he earned working his father's farm. Though the owner's son, his only perks were vegetables and flowers his mother picked from her garden and delivered to them.

Years later, my sister told me everyone had counted months when her first child was born. They thought she had to get married. She said, she did have to get married, but only to get out from under my mother's rule.

I thrived on the attention Marg and Vin gave me. I was not yet seven when she took me along to see the apartment she and Vin would live in after they married. They rented the second floor of a large, yellow, clapboard-house with a turret shaped living room surrounded with windows. It was there, in the empty apartment, she tried on her white satin wedding dress especially for me, as if she required my approval. Vin wasn't allowed to see.

"This is like a story book house," I said. "It must cost lots of money."

"No. It was the cheapest thing we could find, and I think that's why." Marguerite pointed across the street to the Woodland Cemetery. "Lots of people don't want to live near dead people."

We decided that was why the apartment was haunted. Often at night as it was getting dark, you could hear footsteps coming up the front hall stairs. My sister insisted the ghost was a woman, a lonely and shy one. Vin would go to the door and yell into the hall. "You came to get Rosie did you? She can't go out, but come in. Sit down. Have a cup of tea." He'd pretend he could see her, pour her tea. "She's not a bit shy with me," he'd say to my sister and me who by now were doubled with laughter.

I cherished every moment I spent with them no matter where they lived. Their love for each other was enviable. A terrifying loneliness I didn't understand engulfed me after she married. She must have known. She was the sibling I felt the most connected to, as my brothers seemed closer to each other. I wanted to be connected to them also, but they didn't seem to care. Yet we were experts at hiding our feelings — so who knows.

Vin came by and picked me up so I could spend weekends with them. Their apartment smelled of soap, wax and new furniture. Wedding gift tablecloths, not oil cloth, were used even on her kitchen table. Lamps, not glaring overhead lights. Chintz and ruffles. Even after her children were born, her home reflected care and warmth. She parented me along with her own.

On Saturdays, Marguerite and I would push the baby carriage to the library where she picked out books for me. Books she knew I would love like *Sisters*, *Helen's Babies*, and *Daddy Long Legs*. She gave me many a gift — but this one — the habit of reading, I still have. Reading and radio were the only recreation the young couple could afford.

After she died, my brother and I lamented her passing. "Marguerite had class," Harry said, "When I was a kid, she took me all the way into Boston from Revere, because I was dying to see a movie. I think I was her favorite."

I remember feeling betrayed. "You weren't her favorite, I was," I wanted to say. But I didn't. At that moment, I realized the huge capacity this sister had for love. How wonderful that we all felt we were her favorites.

Every Christmas they'd go into debt for their children's toys. Their house was always full of people. It was a warm place for me to be, and my children felt the same. Any confused soul in need of a respite, or any ill relative who needed nursing, Marg and Vin were there. It must have been hard for Vin to live in the shadow of my sister's giving. Often Vin looked "less than" when, for her sake, he tried to curtail her impulsive generosity. I'd side with him when her generosity left them without. My pragmatic mother chastised Marguerite for giving what she couldn't afford. They brought four children into the world — then they adopted a fifth, Michael, the son who served them best as they aged.

"Don't come looking to borrow from me next time," my mother would say but she never turned her down when she needed money for food. Once Vin and Marg came to visit me in Maine after my son was born and brought him an outrageously expensive gift. Then, I had to buy their bus tickets back to Massachusetts, but welcomed the chance to do something for them.

Her giving, and her meticulous housekeeping habits, took their toll on her health. By age 42, overweight and diabetic, she had been diagnosed with a serious heart condition. Sheer love of those around her, her outstanding sense of humor, and her interest in every living thing, kept her alive until she was 72.

My sister's eyes would light up when I visited. She often said she lived her lost youth through mine.

"I've been offered a job in Washington, with the War Department but Dad doesn't want me to go to D.C. He says I'm too young."

Her feet swollen, stomach bursting with the pregnancy of her fourth child, she was still ironing her children's clothes for school after supper.

"No matter what Ma and Dad say, you go. Much as I love Vin and these kids, I wish I had more freedom and education before I got married."

Margaret and Marguerite for some reason were never close. But Marg and I had a mystical relationship. One would pick up the phone and know it was the other. She'd call me just as my mind processed her name, or as I picked up an object she gave me. Apart, we'd select the same books to read. Vin, God bless him, never resented our relationship. He nursed her magnificently in her last days, and when I told him how much I appreciated this he said, "I'd do it forever if I could keep her alive." For three years after her death, over his children's protests, he visited her grave every day, rain or shine, until his Honda broke down and he had to rely on someone to take him.

Shortly before she died, as we sat across from her sick bed, she lifted her head off the pillow and looked outside and said to her daughter and me,

"Look, kids. There's a circus in the backyard! Hear the music! The elephants are parading around the big tent. What beautiful red and gold costumes the riders are wearing."

"Mum, I hate to tell you but there is no circus. It's the medication," my heartbroken niece told her quietly.

My sister, turned to the two of us from her sick bed and laughed,

"I feel sorry for you two. You're missing this great performance. It's so much fun and I didn't even have to pay a cent to see it. Lucky me."

My niece and I looked at each other. We knew who the lucky ones were.

Frank's Way

My brother Frank made his drawing table from tonic cases and discarded lumber. I can picture him now, a shock of blonde hair falling over his face and work space. With pencil, and then crayon, skillfully he drew the future. I sat at his elbow awed by his talent, devouring his every word.

"Man will get to the moon in our lifetime," this older brother said in 1932, as he handed me a sketch of a man in a cone-shaped capsule, positioned behind a steering wheel and dashboard. A yellow shirted pilot is encased in a red rocket. Sparks shoot from the rocket's pointed tail. Behind him, stars fill the dark blue space of the Universe.

"All we need is the right fuel to get us up there. It's not that far to travel."

"God doesn't want us on the moon or we'd been born there," I said, drawing on my seven years of maturity and my new friendship with God. You see, I had just made my First Holy Communion.

My mother wasn't as impressed with Frank's talent.

"You draw and read all day. It's summertime. Go out and play." Frank spent hours pouring over *Popular Mechanics*. I heard her whisper to my father: "He's so unlike our other boys."

"What's so wrong about books and motors?" my father said. He managed a fleet of trucks and his idea of fun was tuning up a car on his day off.

Frank, and his friend Joe Mantini, built the body of an airplane in the large basement of our house in Revere. I think the plan came out of his *Popular Mechanics*. My father dredged up parts from junkyards. "Keeps them busy," he told my mother. Harry and John, my other brothers scoffed, at the grease covered teenagers, but a pilot from the local airport, where Frank spent his free time, didn't laugh.

"It's unbelievable," the pilot said to my father, "These kids have built something that might get off the ground."

Then came the big day. Frank and Joe were thirteen and fourteen, respectively. The plane's fuselage, covered with a heavy, silver fabric that looked like both tin and oil cloth, glistened in the morning sunlight. It was to come out of the basement and wheeled into the garage my father built. There, the wings, rudder and propeller would be attached. Everyone, including Frank's pilot friend, gathered. Excitement filled the air. Then, the two kids pushed it over the threshold of the cellar door and a wheel caught on the doorframe. The fuselage tipped and crashed. The weight of the motor or engine collapsed the structure. The silver covering tore. Frank sat on the back steps and cried. The first time in years. Despite Joe's willingness to begin again, and despite my father's encouragement, Frank never again touched any part of the wreckage.

Shortly afterward, Frank stopped speaking to me. He was drawing at his desk and told me not to look. When he left to go downstairs to our only bath, I looked and was pleased. There they were. The paper dolls I had asked him to draw for me. He had even drawn umbrellas, handbags, and shoes. "They're wonderful," I said when he came back to his desk. He looked at me with hate-filled eyes, and then ripped the page into pieces.

"I'll never speak to you again. Stay away from me." I had spoiled the surprise he had planned for me. I ran to my mother in tears. "Don't mind your brother Frank," she said, "That's Frank's way. He's an odd one." For one childish mistake, he didn't speak to me for years. It hurt something awful.

We moved from that house in Revere to Somerville where Frank graduated from high school. Short, small boned, blonde and shy, he looked about twelve. When he couldn't find a job any better than delivering telegrams for Western Union by bicycle, he joined FDR's Conservation Corps. Muscular and mannish when he finished his CCC stint, he tried to enlist in the Air Corps, but was offered the infantry.

Stationed at Boston Harbor, Frank came home frequently, but he was not a talker. When he hadn't come home on pass for a while, Patrick said, "He's got a girl."

One morning, the Military Police appeared at our front door and told us Frank was Absent Without Leave. By now, our country was at war. This was a serious offense. My parents were devastated. The Military Police soon located Frank, placed him under arrest, and put him in the brig. It was a matter of principle, Frank said.

Seems Frank's barracks commander urged all his men to contribute to the Red Cross so he would achieve one hundred per cent.

"I asked him point blank, 'Is it voluntary?'" Frank said. He had hurt our parents so much that he had to explain.

"Oh yes, but I want 100 percent," said Frank's commander. "A small donation will do."

"I wouldn't give the Red Cross five cents," Frank said. The Salvation Army comes around and gives us everything for nothing. The Red Cross charges us a nickel for coffee or a doughnut and then they want to pose for pictures while they're doing it. My buddies admired my courage, but I was the only one who refused to give. To punish me, he made everyone in my barracks scrub everything in sight with toothbrushes and forced me sit idly on the bunk and watch."

Frank lit a cigarette, puffed, and continued.

"It wasn't just the barracks cleaning; he stalked me, gave me Kitchen Patrol every day, latrine duty every night. I fell into my bunk exhausted, but I still wouldn't donate. A few guys praised me for standing up to him, but most of them wouldn't speak to me. He canceled my pass every time I was eligible.

"I couldn't take it any longer. This guy was mean. When he threatened to hurt me physically, I took off."

After that, Frank tried again to get into the Air Corps. To get away from the Commander, he joined the paratroopers. It must have bothered him when Harry, older than both of us, made cadet training and then 1st Lieutenant. Harry ducked flak and flew supplies from London to the European front while Frank was AWOL. Harry wrote Frank, accused him of lacking patriotism. Said he disgraced the family. I dashed off a scolding letter to Harry, saying Frank wasn't exactly Benedict Arnold. Harry never forgave me for defending Frank.

As a paratrooper, Frank participated in "D" day. Unlike Harry who had an English Batman to lay out his clothes for him every day. Though he never said so, we all knew Frank had it rough. When he was discharged at war's end, he withdrew from all of us.

"He won't talk to me," my mother whined when Frank wouldn't come out of his bedroom except for silent meals. "It hurts, doesn't it?" I wanted to say, remembering she had little sympathy for me when Frank wouldn't speak to me.

I think Frank suffered a postwar depression that was never treated, but marriage did for him what it rarely does: it healed. He married an energetic, winsome woman whose whole life revolved around him. Ruthie's nurturing restored him. Working as a musician, he arranged for both piano and guitar. When Ruthie was expecting a baby, we felt he needed to earn more. He was still designing, writing music and toying with black and white photography, but everyone, except Ruthie, felt he should be pounding the pavement looking for a second job.

"You need more than you have to bring a baby up," my mother said, "Be realistic."

"We've got everything, Ma. Shelter, food, clothing, love for each other. That's all any kid needs," Frank said. My mother shook her head as she left their curtain-less apartment.

When their son Bunky, officially named Charles after a musician friend, was born, Frank changed. He enrolled in school to study electronics and quit because he knew more than the teacher. He got a steady job in that field and never missed a day.

When they could, they bought an inexpensive four-room house. Their bedroom was piled high with wooden shelves he built to store electronic equipment, his photo lab, his guitar, and stacks of paper related to all of the above. Ruthie, God bless her, never complained. Frank was still designing. Darker blonde hair now dipped into his work over another homemade bench in their bedroom. Only now, a cigarette burned in an ashtray beside him.

Before the advent of transistors or chips, he built a one tube TV when ten was the custom. Ruth could do crazy things like turn on lights from a distance or start the coffee from bed. This was startling in the fifties. Everyone told him to apply for patents, but he never did. Fellow musicians played his piano and guitar arrangements for free. He only cared about creating the work.

By contrast, Harry, the former pilot, now living in California, had a Japanese gardener, a big house and a lucrative job in sales. After he saw Frank's house, he forever referred to him as "The Mole". It's okay, because Frank referred to him as the "Bullshit Artist". We all wanted the big suburban house, custom made draperies and two cars. Not Frank. He had everything.

Ruth and Bunky showed up for family First Communions, Confirmations and graduations. Frank didn't. He only went to work. Maybe because he was nervous driving. At home, he'd work in his lab, read, strum his guitar, compose music and smoke too many cigarettes and drink beer. But his head would lift and he'd smile when we stopped by on a Friday or Saturday night. He'd come to the kitchen table, where now we all sipped beer, smoked cigarettes, and ate the popcorn or snacks Ruthie prepared. Now that I look back, he may have suffered panic attacks.

He'd love to argue current events and when he disagreed with me, he'd say, "Is that so Ye Olde Homely

Philosopher?" just to irk me.

We'd often recall the past, stories about siblings and parents. I loved the one about the night our father came home after drinking wine with Mr. Fusanti who owned a farm near our house in Revere.

My mother was screaming at our father.

"Don't you dare come into this house with alcohol on your breath. No drunkard eats with my children."

My staggering father, whipped the tablecloth, all set for dinner, from the table.

"This is my house, and I'll eat with my children or nobody eats." He was a gentle, sweet man when he was sober.

About then, we were sent to our rooms to avoid the ugliness. It was Frank's idea to tie bedclothes together and put them out the second story window. We were going to shimmy down them so we could look in the screen door and see what was going on. Luckily, the argument was short-lived. My mother chased my father out the door threatening him with a broom. We laughed in adulthood, but as children, we were frightened.

Frank and Ruthie's small home was a joy to visit. They shared anything they had. They cared for my mother in her last stages of cancer. It was where my mother preferred to be. Bunky gave up his room for her and slept on the living room couch.

Frank never discussed his war experiences, but he had definite opinions on army or government stupidity. He reminisced about some of the great guys he had met, but we never knew what he went through.

A cynic and critic, his pessimism was often on target. Annoyingly knowledgeable, he read something once and he knew it. You had to do your homework if you wanted to argue with him. He had a tendency to remove the gold polish from everything and showed us the mottled brass underneath.

"Why are you watching that guy?" he said, as his five year old son, Bunky, and I watched Brother Bob, a Boston children's TV celebrity. "You can tell he really hates kids." Brother Bob's irritation with children suddenly became obvious to me and later I learned from someone who worked at the radio station that Frank was right.

Of Arthur Godfrey, he said, "You can't tell me this guy is sweet and affable; I bet he's a bastard to work for."

According to Frank, Ray Charles never would have made it big time if he hadn't been black and blind, and Liza Minelli had an ordinary voice, but Judy Garland for a mother. I never see these stars that I don't think of my brother.

Our family was against the war in Vietnam, but I marched in demonstrations, my sister and I wrote letters to President Johnson, but Frank sat at his kitchen table, drank his Narragansett Ale™, and merely railed against the system.

"What good would it do?" Frank said, when I suggested he write letters of protest. "America is there protecting France's interests. Politics. That's what it's all about."

Then a shocker. Bunky turned eighteen and enlisted in the army right out of high school and wound up in Vietnam. His father was enraged at first, but then wrote his son daily. The boy, unlike his father, saw the world as the sunny place his mother saw. Then another shocker. The innocent, nineteen-year-old, came home in a box shortly after the Tet Offensive. I knew how I felt. I can't trespass on them to imagine their feelings. To do so would trivialize their pain.

Not knowing I was his aunt, one of his former teachers said at Bunky's wake, "You teach hundreds of children over the years, but there are those like Charles you never forget. This boy's light was far reaching. A joy to be around."

Part of Ruth and Frank died with their charismatic only child. Frank switched from Narragansett Ale™ to whiskey. He drank and smoked heavily. Ruth fought harder to survive. Grief separated them for about a year.

"Where was he when I needed him most?" she cried. I thought their marriage was done for. Frank was the one who begged for Ruth's forgiveness. Knowing his stubbornness, I realized how much he loved this wife who did take him back. I visited them in California where they moved for a new start. They seemed closer than ever. Now they had a conventionally lovely home and two poodles. My sister Margaret's son who lived nearby became a frequent visitor. He filled a need as they became his surrogate parents.

Their few good years ended, when Frank was

diagnosed with cancer and couldn't work. Ruthie's office manager job supported their household and not once did anyone hear her complain. Over a period of five years or so his cancer spread to other parts of his body. In the last stages of the disease, he called me and said they were moving to Florida.

"She'll be able to afford to live there comfortably after I'm gone if I sell this house." he said, "California is too pricey." I fought back tears, stunned by his frankness and courage.

I visited them in their new home in Florida about six months before he died. His false teeth were too large for his face, his legs had withered and were lost in a pair of hand tooled cowboy boots he bought on the West Coast that I mentioned were incongruous for a "cool cat".

"Maybe I'm making a statement in memory of the good guys; Tom Mix, Roy Rogers, Gene Autry. I wanted to grow up and be a hero just like them."

As children in the 1930s, if we could scrape up three dimes, Frank walked Patrick and me two miles to a Saturday matinee at the Broadway Theatre in Revere. Movies then inspired more goodness than a church sermon.

The cancer had wracked Frank's body but not his mind. He ranted against Florida traffic patterns, high prices, and stupid restaurants that put too much food on the plates. It was so good to hear.

I noticed they had new furniture. His collection of jazz records, books, tools and mementos of their son

Bunky were all they carried with them.

After Frank died, Ruth showed me his work shed — the walls, shelves and workbench had all been set up again.

"It was here he built me my entertainment center a few months before he died." The shelves were covered with photo equipment. He worked strictly in black and white.

I picked up his tripod with a flash attachment he designed that made perfect sense. Sadness engulfed me as I held and admired it.

"I bet if Frank went to public school today, he wouldn't feel like such an odd ball. He'd have been a design engineer and made a fortune."

"Maybe," Ruth said, "But he had no desire to be successful in business."

"Success would have built his confidence," I said.

Ruth shook her head. "Money was no incentive. He could never compromise. Too honest. That's why your brother was so special."

Frank died rich. Ruth now has all the comforts Frank wanted only for her sake, but she would prefer less — if only she had the two people she loved the most. Her memories are the most valuable things she owns.

Requiem for Harry

It seemed fitting that my brother Harry died playing cards. He played eighteen holes of golf at his Country Club near his home in California, had lunch, then joined a few friends in a card game. His friends said he went to the men's room and when he didn't return, one player, a physician, decided to check on him. It appeared Harry was on his way back to the game when he had a fatal heart attack and fell to the floor. Just like that! Seventy-eight years young. My vital, energetic brother was gone.

Knowing him, if he had to die, this would have been his preference. Some people live to be seventy-eight and spend their last days drooling saliva in a nursing home or in excruciating pain in a hospital bed. The angels my dear departed mother assigned to each of us hovered over Harry and carried his spirit away while he was doing what he loved, playing golf and cards. He was even lucky in death.

To the rest of us, the news came as a shock. More

fit than most of us, he weighed the same as he had at thirty. Never smoked. Only drank wine with dinner. He didn't even drink while he was in the service during World War II. He walked two miles every other day, played golf on alternate days, limited himself to two boiled eggs a week, cereal and fruit for breakfast, drank one cup of black coffee, ate a dry turkey sandwich for lunch and a dinner the size of the one Tony Lasorta hyped in those old TV ads. Damn it! We expected him to live forever.

Growing up, he was my big brother the card player. He played whist in the parish hall of Santa Lucia (Saint Lucy) Catholic Church in Revere, Massachusetts on Thursday nights. It was said, he beat the housedresses off the other players. Most of the whist players were women.

We lived in a neighborhood surrounded by Italian immigrant families. The women called him, "Harry Buck and A Half". It must have had something to do with a bet he made.

The women are unforgettable. Mrs. Rubino, for instance, a heavy woman with a hearty laugh, black thick lustrous hair pulled back into a doughnut. Full, pink-splotched cheeks, beetle colored eyes and naked fine pored skin that glowed like an Ivory Soap ad. She ran the grocery store around the corner from where we lived. Something about her anatomy forced the home made cotton dresses she wore to rise up in the back and dip down in front. As opposed to most of the people in the neighborhood, Mrs. Rubino spoke English well.

"Hey, Rosa. Tell your broder, I'ma gonna get even tonight," she'd say, smiling when I went into the store to buy the fresh loaves of round white Italian bread my mother treated us to once a week. "Harry Buck-An-A-Half beata me for the last time." One neighbor was called Johnny Lemona and Lima because he sold citrus in Haymarket Square.

During the week when he'd see Mrs. Rubino, or Mrs. Martini, another whist player, he'd grin wide and mischievously. Wearing a knitted sailor's watch cap set off on the back of his head, he'd yell across the street at them.

"Don't forget, Ladies. Bring lots of money next Thursday." Sometimes he'd speak English, sometimes Italian.

"This time, I'll geta even wida you," Mrs. Rubino would yell holding a fat clenched fist mid-air. Mrs. Martini would grin from ear to ear.

Either lucky or smart, Harry usually won. Smart enough to pick up the neighborhood Sicilian dialect, he won the respect of our neighbors, but not my mother. He was still in high school when he'd offer her his winnings from whist, and although we were in the throes of the Depression, she not only refused to take his winnings, she scolded him.

"I pray God, you straighten out. Playing cards is gambling." She would wring her hands anxiously. "You want to grow up and be some kinda 'Big Shot'?

"Big Shot" may have commanded respect from the impressionable young men who lived in that neighborhood, but not from their mothers. The Italian mothers would tell my mother their biggest fear was that their sons would be influenced by older men who made their living booking numbers or doing odd jobs for people they called "the syndicate". Big shots drove new cars and wore fancy suits, jewelry, and pointed toe shoes. These men wouldn't be caught dead playing cards with middle aged housewives in the parish hall. My mother worried just the same.

I remember the house in then rural Revere as the finest of the seven we lived in. Parquet floors, French doors, lots of windows, a large backyard. Five bedrooms accommodated seven children and Grandpa. My sister Marguerite married from there. Baby Vincent had died and the oldest, Arthur, married before we even moved to Revere. We loved our Italian neighbors, especially their cooking, but we knew we were considered the inept Irish who ate lousy soft bread and canned food because we didn't know how to grow things. But how they respected Harry.

After Harry graduated from high school, we lost that house. My father lost his job and the bank foreclosed on our mortgage. We moved back to the city where we lived in a bank owned flat in Somerville. Harry soon found more card players. He joined a "For Men Only" club whose members wore awful teal blue rayon shirts. Across the back of the shirt, embroidered in yellow floss was the word "Troubadours". I don't think they made music.

Once, my mother sent me to the club to get him. Timidly, I knocked. The glass window of the unmarked store front door was heavily curtained. A middle-aged man peeked out and then opened the door. The smell of tobacco and pungent tomato sauce wafted by me. Behind him, I could see the smoke mid-air and the puffing card players. When I asked for Harry, the man said in Italian, *spata minuta*. Thanks to my Revere background, I recognized this as "wait a minute". When Harry came to the door, I could tell he was annoyed.

"Tell her I'll be home when I finish this hand." He said it like he was the boss, but he feared my mother's wrath as much as I did. He knew he'd better come home. In my eleven-year old mind, I imagined my brother was involved in some clandestine operation. I later learned that "Men Only" clubs are a European tradition. I bet my brother was the one of a few, or the only, Irish member. Either he loved cards or Italians. Maybe both.

For Harry, and the rest of my siblings, college was out of the question. He drove a truck for a small automotive spring company, and according to my mother, his salary sustained our family in the late thirties. She gave him a weekly allowance and I think he multiplied it playing cards at the club. He paid me a quarter a week to shine his shoes. He knew I could go to two double feature movies for that money in those days.

Of all my mother's children, I think she enjoyed Harry the most. I'm not saying she loved him more, but he could lift her from the doldrums of poverty faster than anyone. He got away with more than any of us because in the middle of her fury, he'd lift her out of a chair and dance her around the kitchen, and soon she'd be laughing.

World War II impacted all our lives. Frank enlisted before the war because he couldn't find work. The minute war broke out, Harry enlisted so he could select the branch of the service he wanted. He was accepted as a cadet in the Army Air Corps. Later as a 2nd Lieutenant, based in England, he was awarded the Distinguished Flying Cross. He flew 35 missions in a B 24. Frank chose the Infantry but later transferred to the Paratroopers. My brother John joined the Merchant Marine. We hung a three-star rayon-silk panel in our window and prayed the minute we learned they hit foreign soil. They all did. Patrick, too young for World War II, did hard service in Korea later.

Sad as it seems, it took the War to elevate the financial status of most Americans. Labor in demand, my father got a decent job. I had no trouble getting a job in the Telephone Company and from there, I was recruited to work in Washington, D.C. for the U. S. Signal Corps. Even my mother left her own kitchen to cook in another.

Harry's life in the Air Corps broadened his proverbial horizon. He had been dating a local Italian girl, but while in the service he met and fell in love with Donnie, a woman with dark hair and flawless skin, who looked like Joan Crawford. Donnie was a self-employed hairdresser from Crockett, California.

Blessed with height, good looks and a dynamic personality, Harry was a successful in sales. He sold large equipment for Westinghouse Electric and made California his home until he died. If the rest of my family moved from poor to middle class, I'd say Harry moved from poor to upper middle class.

I live on the East Coast, and at a gathering I attended, a man from the West Coast coincidentally worked at Westinghouse Electric in the same division Harry worked.

"Your brother is legendary," he said, "In our company he's top gun, a trail blazer." Like all siblings, who, I guess, feel another's accomplishment reflects on them, I was pleased he was highly esteemed by his peers.

All success is relative. Compared to our parents, all of us children had more material things than they had, but Harry's standard of living was the best and was a source of pride to my parents. How we enjoyed the story he told about my mother and father's first visit to his home in California.

Harry and Donnie's pretentious home was high on a hill facing San Francisco and Mt. D'ablo. A manicured Oriental garden graced the sloping property behind his house. Sitting in a lounge chair on the terrace above one afternoon reading the newspaper, my father spotted a Japanese man picking plants out of the earth.

"Hey, you," my father yelled, as if he was back in Charlestown. He got out of the chair and all six-feet-two of him approached the small man.

"What are you doing here?" he demanded, "This is private property." Harry watched in amusement from inside his house. The Japanese man explained in nervous broken English that he was the hired gardener.

My father applied his favorite expression, "What a long tail my cat has grown." My parents were pleased by Harry's success.

A halo Harry doesn't deserve. Sometimes he exhibited less patience than a three-year-old. And, dear God, wasn't he always right. It was senseless to argue with him. A male chauvinist from the word "woman". A man's idea took precedence over a woman's. As his sister I forgave him, knowing he was raised in the "dark ages" of male-supposed-superiority. If it made him feel secure to think women were dumb, so be it. That was his problem, not mine. Deep down he knew better, as evidenced by the respect for the accomplishments of his wife and daughter, expressed only when they were not around.

We were constantly arguing about my perception of what happened growing up. Born eight years apart, I saw things much differently than he. He said our brother Frank had never worked for Western Union when he got out of high school.

"You're nuts," he said, "Frank never worked a day in his life until he got into the army." And, I'll be damned, he had me believing it until I asked my sister-in-law. She showed me the snapshot of Frank on a bike in uniform with Western Union across his hat. I never got around to mailing it to him. How I loved to one-up Harry.

He was the brother who called home frequently. I married, in 1951 and moved to Maine, but came home weekends to visit my parents who now owned a Mom and Pop store in Charlestown, Massachusetts. Harry telephoned her every weekend and her excitement was obvious.

"You'll have to wait or come back later. It's my son Harry. He's calling all the way from California." She'd walk away from her customers to get to the pay phone, then, shout her conversation across the miles.

He did his best to be a good son, father, brother and husband, as well as a soldier. True to his Irish-Catholic roots, he gave generously to the poor and rooted for the powerless without regard to race or creed. This stewardship was not only based on religion. We often discussed how we were once the recipients of government handouts when my father was unemployed for a year or so in the thirties.

I miss his intelligent letters. His wit and sense of humor. I miss our visits and telephone calls on holidays, when we always picked up where we left off — as if my husband and I had seen him the day before. The conversation may have been controversial, argumentative, but it was always stimulating.

Though he made more money than any of my

brothers, if ever he bragged, it was about what interesting adults his four children had become and for that he gave Donnie the most credit. Before he died he saw his children grow up capable and strong.

Before our mother died, she saw that her prayers for Harry had been answered. The card-playing son had become a "Big Shot" in the best sense of the term. He was as good a citizen as this country ever gets.

The Pretty Sister

Margaret stepped off the bus at the corner as if it were a royal coach. Head raised high, it stretched higher when the cluster of young men, who hung out in front of Jake's Variety, whistled. Women sitting on the stoops of tenements ogled her with envy as she paraded up the street on her way home from what my mother bragged was her white-collar job at Boston City Hall.

A wide-brimmed red straw hat, white puffed-sleeved blouse with navy polka dots, matching navy skirt reversed with white polka dots — the outfit was striking. Especially since she cinched her tiny waist with a wide red leather belt. She resembled, and moved like, the Vogue magazine models she admired.

"Who's that pretty lady?" one of my playmates asked.

"That's my big sister." I responded with pride. We were new in the neighborhood.

Though men were attracted to her, she returned their attention with ridicule and criticism. So it was a big surprise when, twelve years after my sister

Marguerite married, Margaret, destined to remain single according to everyone who knew her, got married at age thirty. Our family had no idea.

Margaret had left home after a tempestuous relationship with my mother. For years, prior to her marriage, she lived alone in a studio apartment in Harvard Square, Cambridge, not far from Harvard College where she worked.

The estrangement began over nonsense. A year after she was hired at City Hall, a new political regime eliminated her job. Since my father was also unemployed, my parents were desperate for income. They did what desperate people do — something foolish. With their small savings, they took over a failing restaurant on First Street in Cambridge based on the fact that my father had once cooked in a Jesuit Seminary. It took him a long time to discover that truck drivers had a different appetite than the Jebbies. The failing restaurant he gave his name failed a lot more before it closed permanently.

While my mother was at Jack's Lunch washing dishes, baking macaroni and cheese and sumptuous apple pies, unemployed Margaret became our surrogate mother. The conflict began.

"Bananas are too high," I heard my mother yell. "I leave you money to buy stuff we need: potatoes, bread, meat and milk not bananas."

"We only use a few. They're nutritious for the children. We're arguing about pennies." Margaret read Good

Housekeeping and Vogue. She knew how to eat and dress properly.

"You didn't save any milk for Harry. He's the only one bringing in money. The kids can get by with less," my mother shouted when she opened the refrigerator. Harry was a deliveryman for a small automotive spring company. He gave my mother his salary.

"That big ox doesn't need it," Margaret yelled back. "The young kids are growing." Margaret and Harry, close in age, were rivals. They went two rounds every morning before breakfast.

Exhausted from the restaurant, my mother was cranky. She had stood on her feet all day. It didn't take much to trigger an argument. Housekeeping was secondary to her. She never appreciated how clean Margaret kept the house. My sister made us remove our shoes at the back door, hang up our coats and put things away. No more piling stuff in a heap on the blanket chest.

Afternoons Margaret sat at the kitchen table, her feet up on another chair, reading women's magazines and eating Nabisco Saltines with Kennedy's peanut butter and sipping tea. Since we got none, we squealed. Margaret caught the dickens.

One snowy day, she locked us out all afternoon so we wouldn't mess the house before my mother got home. I wet my woolen snow pants in the back hall because she had washed the kitchen floor and I couldn't cross it to get to the bathroom. I sat in the cold back hall beside the smelly kerosene barrel until my mother got home. She scolded Margaret when I showed her my chafed inner thighs.

All I know, is I woke up one morning and learned Margaret had left — followed by the words — "for good." This hurt my mother. Years before, an older brother, John, had run away. No one knew where he had gone for a couple of years. No one knew where Margaret had gone either.

Later, a neighbor of my Aunt Kitty's said she ran into Margaret, and found out she had a job at Harvard College. For weeks, my mother sat staring out the kitchen window as if she expected Margaret to come up the backdoor walkway.

I was out of high school, working at my first job, when I saw Margaret again. This time, she ran into a cousin, who told her that I worked in the Telephone Company office not far from where Margaret lived in Harvard Square.

"How about going out to dinner?" she said, when she telephoned. "My treat." Her voice quivered like a boy's did when he calls to ask you for a first date.

"Sure, why not," I said, a little nervous too. After that, I saw her secretly as I had no desire to irritate or hurt my mother. Since she was ten years older than I was, I felt summoned when she called. With so little self-esteem in those days, I felt sorry for anyone who went to such lengths to have dinner with me. Once she took me to Filene's Basement and bought me a fine woolen two-piece dress so I'd have something decent to wear when she took me to posh restaurants like the Fox and Hounds. Before that, all I knew was an annual treat at F. W. Woolworth's lunch counter during the Christmas rush with my mother. Though uncomfortable accepting her generosity, I was also grateful.

"How do you stand living at home?" she asked. "I'm so glad to get out of that messy house." Margaret was so neat she dusted her bedroom curtains daily. "Ma never should have married and had all those kids. She can't handle the responsibility."

We'd argue about my parents, especially my mother. My mother was not easy, but Margaret exaggerated her faults. I'd look around Margaret's small studio apartment and sometimes envy the courage it took for her to leave home. Her place smelled of cinnamon and spice and everything in it was precisely placed. Cafe curtains and a daybed slip covered in a cheerful floral pattern she had made herself. "Feel," she said handing me one of the six matching pillows she had lined up on the daybed. "It's real goose down. I made these myself." I had never heard of down. Its softness against my cheek assured me it was special.

At Sunday lunch before a movie she served me a toasted cheese sandwich, pickle and chips on Quimper® china and poured tea from a matching pot. Blue and white gingham napkins and tablecloth covered the white painted wooden table. Her tiny Harvard Square studio apartment had the feel of a French farmhouse.

My parents weren't into decor in those ten years before the war; they were into survival. Our house teemed with smells of cabbage or mutton cooking. They struggled to keep body, soul and their family whole. At that time, I was able to give them ten of the fifteen dollars salary I earned at the Telephone Company. I couldn't have done what Margaret did. I felt I was betraying them not only by visiting my sister, but also by making unfair comparisons.

"Why didn't they ever encourage us to get an education?" Margaret said. "We were as smart as the Jewish and Italian kids in school who went on to college. Ma and Dad didn't care what kind of jobs we got as long as we paid them board."

What did she expect? My mother had gone to the eighth grade in school, my father the fifth. To them, we were educated. Besides, my mother felt her job was to bring our souls to God. Education was secondary in the divine scheme. She didn't think secular.

Margaret called me at work often. I saw her about twice a year only at times I couldn't come up with a good excuse. So when my mother said Aunt Kitty read her marriage intention in the Sunday Globe, I was shocked. I had spoken to Margaret six months before. She had never mentioned a man.

"Who's this man you gave up your independence for?" I phoned to congratulate her on her marriage later that week.

"Who told you? I thought sure no one would find

out," she said, then went on to describe him. "He seems intelligent, has a pretty good job, and we seem to have a lot in common."

When I asked if she would move, she said she would stay in her studio apartment until they found a larger place.

"We'll have you to dinner, when we have the space." When I hung up I was happy for her, but not for long as the marriage lasted only six months.

Long enough for her to get pregnant. I never did meet Margaret's husband.

"Come see your sister Margaret's baby," my aunt Kitty said on the telephone about a year later. "Sparkling brown eyes just like hers. She's living here, as she has nowhere to go. Her landlord kicked her out when she had the baby. When she called me, I had to take her in."

Aunt Kitty, the youngest of my mother's sisters, had one child and, knowing her I bet it was by choice. I suspected she called me because she was fed up.

When I went to see Margaret and her handsome baby, my aunt pulled me aside.

"I love the baby, and Margaret's paying me a stipend — but I'm getting too old for the commotion — the laundry, the baths, the use of the kitchen. This trouble between your mother and Margaret, don't you think it's time they buried the hatchet?"

I took my aunt's message home to my parents. Before long, my parents told me to approach Margaret and tell her that for all practical purposes she should come home. There was a child to consider.

"Oh no. I'll not play the role of the prodigal daughter returning," Margaret said, standing at the stove stirring a boiling copper vat, with a huge wooden paddle, that held diapers. Perspiration poured down her drawn face. Her thick hair was pulled back in an elastic.

"You see," Aunt Kitty said pointing to Margaret, "It's not enough the diapers were washed in my Easy Washer, and then soaked in bleach, your sister has to boil them." Eventually, Margaret caught on. Aunt Kitty's patience had fizzled.

My mother was gallant. She acted as if nothing had ever happened between mother and daughter. We squeezed two more people into that post war house my parents owned on Ferry Street. My sister insisted on paying board. When neighbors and friends assumed baby Paulie's father was killed during the war, it was left that way.

We all fussed over Margaret's brown-eyed baby with the beautiful disposition. My mother, or one of us, gladly took care of him when she worked as a waitress from 5:00 p.m. to midnight at a downtown Boston hotel. Waitress work, she claimed, was the only job that paid women well. It must have. Soon, she rented the first floor flat of our house. She bought a bed, crib, and couch from Sears on time and gradually furnished the four rooms.

My mother worried because my sister rode the

streetcar after midnight coming from her waitress job.

"You're entitled to Aid for Dependent Children," my mother suggested, "It would be nice if you could spend more time with the baby now, and work when he goes to school."

"I don't take handouts," Margaret snapped indignantly. High strung was the term my mother used to excuse this daughter who bawled her out because the baby got chocolate stains on his bathrobe while in her care. I think, like all mothers, she felt responsible for Margaret's disposition.

Margaret lived with us until she found a house she could afford. A little handyman's special and she became the handy woman. She learned carpentry: put up walls, closets, wallpapered, and tiled her own bath. The only woman I knew who owned a power saw. She had no patience with indolence. Managed money like an accountant and gave a percentage of her income to church and charity. You had to admire her independence and diligence. Everything she purchased was researched. She consumed at the lowest possible price. So practical, she criticized me when I read Hemingway. Fiction was a waste because it wasn't useful.

"Some Squaw," my brother Harry said when he saw how she had remodeled her house.

In our family we all argued, politics, movies, myriad subjects, but Margaret didn't argue like the rest of us. Her positions were truths not to be questioned — sort of like the Baltimore Catechism. If she was thin, we all should be. If she ate organically, than we were eating poison. No wonder we avoided her.

"Poor Margaret. She must be lonely," I said discussing her with my brother Frank.

"Stop feeling sorry for her. Margaret doesn't have any use for what she can't control. She may love someone from afar, but that doesn't mean she wants them around her. She's alone and her life is just the way she wants it."

Frank's assessment proved true as Paulie grew up. A loving mother when he was an infant and young child, she found him difficult when he began to develop his own ideas. So, Margaret sent him to a private Catholic boarding school during high school. He got a partial scholarship.

The second year he was there, the priest in charge called my mother to tell her that her grandson was ill.

"This student said his mother wouldn't allow him to come home and I didn't believe him, but I just hung up with her, and he's right. She refused to come get him. The boy is very ill. He asked me to call you. What kind of a mother is she?" the priest asked.

My mortified mother apologized for my sister and had Patrick, who had five children of his own, pick the boy up at school and drive him to my mother's one-room apartment. My mother got little satisfaction when she called Margaret and scolded her.

"If he's not going to listen to me, he can stay at school."

During his prep school summers, Paul hopped from my house, to my brother's, to my mother's. Margaret was adamant. He was not living with her. We talked to him as if he were the adult, and she the misbehaving child. By the time he was in college, he learned to do what my mother suggested: "Put up with her shenanigans." So he did get to go home summers.

When he did live with his mother one summer, he went on the road selling magazines door-to-door. One day, he rifled through his mother's desk looking for a pen and spotted mail from the Veteran's Administration. He learned his father was still alive and his mother had been receiving an allowance all along because his father was a World War II Veteran. When he confronted her, she became enraged. I knew she didn't want her ex-husband near her son, because she said he was unstable, but I never knew Paul was actually told his father was dead. The boy was furious. They fought constantly after that and when Paul finally left home after college he did find his father six months before the man died.

I think of Margaret as an unconditional spirit trapped in conditions. It's not an original line, I read it somewhere, but it made me think of this sister, who blamed everyone else for her unhappiness. She felt our parents cheated us by not encouraging us to go to college. Her failed marriage was her husband's fault. He was too controlling. The difficulty with her son was his refusal to listen to his mother.

We thought all was well until I invited Margaret and Paul to my house on Thanksgiving. My siblings refused to invite her.

"Paul is home from college but he's not allowed to come with me," my sister said. "He's impossible to get along with. I'll not have him spoil my day."

My mother had died that year on Halloween, 1965. I missed her, but I was happily married and had two small children who needed me. My sister missed her more, though she didn't say so. That Thanksgiving Day, I looked at my once attractive sister with a heart full of pity. At fifty, she looked drab and dowdy. Tense lines around her mouth overshadowed her good looks. Overweight, she dressed like a prison matron and her fingers were beginning to claw from arthritis. At my mother's funeral that year, Margaret gave me a lecture.

"I'm glad I've got weight on me," she said. "You're too thin. You need weight on you. Then if you get ill, your body will have something to feed on, like Ma's did." We had lost her to cancer.

As we sat down to the huge dinner my husband and I had labored over, she started in on my parents' faults. I tried to laugh it off. The word dysfunctional was just coming into vogue. She used it often. I was still raw from losing my mother to her long, painful illness.

"Yes, we are a very functional, dysfunctional family," I said. "Not hot-house cultivated, because we were raised like weeds. Weeds have to be strong to survive. In a way that's good. We made our own choices. As

Ma used to say, thank God no feeble minded among us. All our parents wanted was that we never rode the Paddy wagon and that we were decent human beings."

"Things are different today," she said, firing words rapidly, "I am difficult because I want my son to have a better life than I had." She didn't know I knew she had lied to him about his father's death. "And after all the sacrifices I've made for him, he shows no gratitude. Until he's earning his own living, he's obliged to listen to me. You should hear the way he talks back to me." One fight I knew of was caused by his not making his bed. The boy had a 3.5 average in college. Finally graduated 23rd from the top of his class. She ranted on and on, listing his faults as she once listed my mother's when I visited her Cambridge apartment.

Exasperated by her unreasonableness, after two glasses of wine, I reminded her of her youth.

"They say teenagers are the enemies of their parents. Remember your rebellion," I said calmly, but my face flushed with white wine, "You defied Mum when you were his age. You left home in the middle of the night without so much as a goodbye. You left Mum and Dad in a lurch when they needed you the most."

"They bought that stupid restaurant and I was supposed to take care of their kids. What did they do for me? I wanted to go to dress designing school," she yelled back.

"They gave us nothing because they had nothing." Now I was shouting. "But they gave us everything they had. They sacrificed and they deserved to be thanked. They fed and clothed eight children and to do that, they did whatever they could to eke out a living. Including that stupid restaurant. What's more, they helped needy strangers. In their own way, they were quite remarkable." I hadn't known what I felt until that moment. My husband and children looked at me as if I were a stranger. I had upset them.

The rage was written on her face. She was pale and speechless. The good natured kid sister was not supposed to speak up. She never came again.

Thanks to my brother Harry's intervention, about five years before Margaret died of colon cancer, at age eighty, she reconciled with her son. They hadn't seen each other for about twenty years. Unmarried and very successful, he could have done much to help make his mother's life easier if she had allowed him into her life earlier.

For twenty-five years after that Thanksgiving Day, whenever I saw her at a family gathering, I'd walk right up to her, and greet her with a bold "hello". Silence. Then, she would turn away. I offered no apology. What I had said that Thanksgiving was true. It worked out fine for me. I felt a freedom from her psychological tyranny. I was glad she didn't speak to me.

For years, out of pity, I had invited her to my home and she had always managed to spoil our holiday celebrations by her harsh criticisms of us or other family members. Not that she would have accepted, but

I no longer felt obliged to invite her for Thanksgiving or Christmas dinner. Our holidays were more relaxing as we didn't have to worry about carefully choosing our words.

I soon discovered how nicely she survived without my holiday invitation. She found others to dine with — not relatives, but people she obviously couldn't hurt as easily, nor were they likely to hurt her.

How vain I was all those years to think my big sister Margaret needed me.

Last One to Wed

The bell tingles, the heavy door slams, I hear Mame Kelly's high-pitched voice. The sounds wake me as I sleep on the daybed in the sitting room behind my parents' small variety store. At first I forget where I am.

"Morning Margaret, is the milk in yet?" Mame asks. Some of my mother's friends call her Peg, some call her Maggie as my father does, Mame calls her Margaret.

"He's late," my mother replies, "But he'll be along any minute now."

Their voices travel through the open transom into the three-bedroom apartment that came with the store. In 1950, my parents sold our big house in Everett and bought the business when my father's arthritis caused him to stop working as a truck mechanic. Cold cement floors had aggravated his rheumatoid condition.

"Keep your voice down, Rose is still sleeping. Jack picked her up at North Station last night at 11:00. Poor child. Covered with coal soot from the Boston and Maine."

"Down for the wedding, is she?" Mame poses the question knowing the answer. Mame knows I am here today for my brother Patrick's wedding at 3 o'clock. Mame was crushed because she and Dan weren't invited. We have so many relatives, my mother felt friends were an imposition since the bride's parents were holding the reception at home. Mame and my parents have been friends for years since their earlier days in Charlestown.

"Rose's husband couldn't come," my mother says. "He had to work."

"That's right, she's the daughter married to the big-shot hotel manager in Maine."

I hear my mother's apology for my absent husband. Her words are true. He simply couldn't get away. Had to oversee someone else's wedding reception.

"Poor guy," my mother says, "He works hard, six or seven days a week."

"Those foreigners are used to that, Mame says," and then asks, "Where's Jack?"

"Gone down to Dutton's to get those cinnamon rolls Rose loves."

Now when I visit, my folks treat me like a guest. Before I left home, no one went to a store to get anything special for me. I love the attention. The truth is, it's my brother Frank who loves the cinnamon coffee rolls, not me. I'm a sucker for jelly doughnuts. But I don't tell my parents.

The bell tingles again. I think it's Mame leaving, but it's my father back from the bakery. I hop out of bed, grab my robe, skirt empty milk cases to go through the kitchen to get to the bathroom. I see someone has lit the copper gas boiler to heat the water for our baths. Their shower is a ring contraption over the tub. The plastic curtain clings to my buttocks as I wash away the residue of soot I slept in the night before.

My father knocks on the bathroom door, shouts above running water. "How do you want your eggs?"

"One egg over lightly." The coffee smells familiar. No one makes coffee like my father. He puts eggshells in with the grinds, says they absorb the acid. It tastes great. My mother minds the store while Dad and I catch up over a two-egg, bacon, and cinnamon roll breakfast. I had my gabfest with my mother the night before. Up past midnight talking, she brought me up to date — talked about Patrick and his bride-to-be, Edie. Since I live in Maine, I met Edie only once. "The girl seems nice," my mother assured me, "Patrick is happy."

I wish Patrick, my youngest brother, happiness. This brother never hurts anyone intentionally. If he does, someone else is responsible. One of Pat's army buddies in Korea was married to Edie's sister. Edie consoled him through the mail after an undeserving girl wrote Patrick a Dear John letter. They liked each other in correspondence: loved each other in person Patrick is the fourth of my brothers to serve the armed forces during a war.

As I devour the eggs I didn't want, my Dad tells me how much he has won on the horses at Suffolk

Downs that week. I feign interest, knowing he never reports losses.

My parents have only one day a week away from the store. My mother insists they can't leave together. On her day off, she takes the subway to Boston with my Aunt Nora to browse or shop. Always they attend Mass at the Franciscan Chapel on Arch Street at noon.

On my father's day off from the store, if the season is open, he drives to one of the horse racing tracks in New England. If not, he lunches at a local bar where he places bets with a bookie. My father is no big-time gambler. "A City Hall" better, the bookies call him. Bets two dollars per race. He can tell you the parentage and performance of any horse running from Pimlico to Suffolk. People seek him out for this.

Meanwhile, Mame still gossips with my mother. Tells her Dennehy was drunk last night and raised hell in the stairway of her three-story house. She called the cops. They shut him up. I know Dennehy through my parents. A red-haired, freckled, often out-of-work longshoreman with eight kids. I tell my mother that if I were Dennehy's wife, I'd be the one drinking. Mame's husband Dan drinks more than the lot of them, but Mame pretends she doesn't notice. She concentrates on her spotless home and starched housedresses, and everyone else's weaknesses.

I dress early for the wedding. After my huge breakfast, I will skip lunch. At a 3 o'clock wedding there is usually no Mass. I expect it will be brief. I plan to eat at the reception.

"You look nice," my mother says. Her compliments are minimal so I know she likes my Wedgwood silk shirtwaist dress. "Here," she says, handing me one of my father's gray shopcoats. "Put this on. It'll keep you clean." I feel six years old. As their youngest daughter, I have little power when I am around my family.

"Who will mind the store while we're gone?" I ask. My mother has a long-standing rule, we never close the store. She fears if they close the store, the elderly Jewish couple who own another variety store across the street, will steal her customers. Though I don't argue with my mother, I think this is pretty far-fetched. First of all, Bunker Hill Street is wide and heavily traveled; crossing it is life threatening. The Goodmans' customers come from the densely populated streets off Bunker Hill Street behind their store, and my parents' business comes from people who live on streets on their side. Secondly, my parents' store is in a predominately Irish-Catholic neighborhood noted for its bigotry, and in my parents' store window, among the display cans of Campbell Soup and fake Wonder Bread, stands a three-foot statue. It replicates the apparition of Our Lady at Lourdes. In the rocky-arched Grotto, the Virgin, hands clasped in prayer, looks piously over any passerby. The fake stones in the arch are cemented together with fluorescent paint. A bulb below lights a pool of fake water in front of the statue. It shines on the grotto stones and renders them green and purple.

It's ugly enough to make me wish I were a Baptist.

I often look over at the Goodmans' with sympathy. Two small elderly people who remind me of characters from Bernard Mallard's, *The Assistant*. They sit on tonic cases outside their store under the green and white striped awning waiting for kids to buy slush or penny candy. I want to warn them, the Virgin is tough to beat. My mother is truly religious, but she is also, much to the surprise of my siblings, one sharp cookie. Ironically, the competing shopkeepers are friendly. It is too expensive for both stores to stock their customers' every need. They commiserate when they borrow product from each other.

"Kids today, I dunno, they steal eyes from your head," Mr. Goodman says. "You gotta watch all the time."

"I know. But it's the fifties," my mother says. "Parents don't make their kids behave like we did."

Now, I repeat my earlier question. "Who will mind the store?"

"A friend of Mame's, Josephine, is coming. Josephine badly needs money," she explains.

I find myself in charge of logistics. "We ought to be ready to leave at 1:45 p.m. if the wedding is at 3:00 p.m." At my suggestion, my mother takes her bath. I roll the bangs of her permed hair in curlers before she bathes. Finally, she appears corseted and slim in a new floral dress. She waits on customers, new dress, curlers and all. No apron or shopcoat for her as she scoops ice cream into cones.

My father is stocking shelves. My mother and I urge him to get dressed.

"Can't you see I'm busy?" Annoyed, he shouts at my mother, not me, I'm the guest. I'm told an older sister, Margaret, will drive us all to the wedding. Patrick has provided her with the map and directions to the church.

"What time is Josephine coming?" I ask. Now, my mother calls to my father and repeats my question.

My father comes out of the back room smelling of the Old Spice I gave him for Christmas.

"Why ask me?" he says, adjusting his tie. "You made all the arrangements."

My mother looks at him hard. "I told you to call Mame and have her ask Josephine to come," she shrills.

"I did," says my father. "But I thought you had arranged the details."

"Call Mame," my mother screams, pointing her arm like a rifle at the phone booth beside the front door. She mumbles to me about the unreliability of my father. He crosses the oiled-wood floor to the booth, but not before my parents continue their customary game of you said, I said, and no I didn't say.

My father telephones Mame because it seems Josephine doesn't have a telephone. Mame has to go next door to get her. Mame has told Josephine to get there at 2:15 p.m. Mame tells my father that she was thinking St. Ann's in Waltham, not the faraway

St. Ann's way down in Weymouth. But how could she know when she never got an invitation.

About then, Margaret, the family CEO, arrives with her ten-year-old son, who likes to go in and out of the store to hear the bell.

"Stop doing that," Margaret scolds. "Get back in the car."

"Why do you still have curlers in your hair?" she asks. No hello. This is the first thing she says to our mother.

In our distress, we have overlooked this fact. I take my now agitated mother out back to comb her hair and put on her makeup. She relates every mistake my father has made in the past year. When I'm through, she still looks angry, but somewhat better. Margaret doesn't know that this is not our only delay, but we soon hear her response when my father says we have to wait for Josephine. "What! she shouts." You could have heard her down in Sullivan Square.

She marches into the backroom to scold my mother. "Why couldn't you have just closed the damn store? So you lose ten bucks." Her hands wave midair. "Your last child is getting married for God's sake. Thank God, Patrick is sleeping at Frank's. He'd be nuts about now." I agree, but remain silent. Margaret's outrage suffices.

Mame comes in gasping for breath as she speaks. Like my parents, she is in her sixties. "Egad, Josephine lives on the third floor. She's coming right away. I'm sorry, if only I got an invitation, I would have known."

A half-dressed Josephine arrives at 2:10 p.m. We all

stand in front of the store waiting for her. We pile into Margaret's Volkswagen. My Dad sits up front to help navigate. One right turn instead of a left cost us ten more minutes. Margaret wasn't listening — too busy sputtering about how my parents never get anything straight because they are so busy bickering. My knuckles are white; she drives her brake, even on Route 128. We finally find St. Ann's. We pull up to the church as the bride and groom come down the front stairs under a confetti storm. I can't believe it. The wedding is over! We have missed the twenty-two minute ceremony.

The youthful couple glow. He is tall, broad shouldered — she is small, such a tiny waist — their smiles seem wider than their bodies. They almost trip on the church stairs looking into each other's eyes. When we get out of the car, Patrick sees us and shakes his head smiling. He is too happy to allow our late arrival to spoil his day.

At the reception, he never asks why, but Margaret feels obliged to explain whose fault it was. He laughs, and says, typical. Margaret insists it is not funny, she is mortified in front of all these people. The reception is nothing fancy but a good time. Plenty of food and drink to celebrate. Each family tells the other the wonderful qualities of the child given in matrimony on that day. My parents act as if nothing has happened.

On the way home, Margaret starts harping again. My parents never say a word in their own defense. I'm the one who says,

"Margaret, please, that's enough."

The car now seems empty. Only once after that does anyone speak. My father turns to my mother in the back seat, taps her knee to get her attention and says,

"I forgot to tell you how nice you looked today, Maggie." She smiles coyly, flushes and says,

"G'wan, with you, I'm too fat."

Maggie and Jack

My father used to say, "Put a dollar sign in front of any number and your mother's brain becomes an abacus."

At the two-aisle pre-war A & P store, the clerk would gather my mother's groceries one by one, set them on the polished wooden counter, then tabulate the cost of each item in pencil on a brown paper bag. Along to help carry her bags, I burst with pride every time my mother Maggie, with nothing but an eighth grade education, stuns the clerk.

"Three dollars and twenty-eight cents after you deduct the four cent deposit for the two Cliquot Club tonic bottles I returned." The poor man would still be carrying sums to the second column when she'd give him the total.

To a mill, my mother could tell any inquirer, what we spent on heat, food or rent, annually. If she had the proper education, she'd have made an excellent candidate for Wharton's School of Business. You might conclude she was money-minded because she had little as a child, but my father who lived the quintessential Dickens' childhood, had little respect for money — unless he was without it. He bought on impulse and was generous without investigation. A dreamer, and a sometime alcoholic, he felt his job was to please, and make people happy.

Jack to his wife and friends, Pa to his sons and Dad to his daughters, my father was a thoughtful generous man. He brought home gadgets to lighten his wife's workload. Maggie would scold, remind him we couldn't afford an electric roaster when the rent was overdue.

He'd tell her he bought it because their old friend Fitzie just got a job at Creedon's Hardware and needed to make an impression on his boss. The yellow enamel roaster, too small for a family of eight, was used a couple of Sundays and soon found its way to the back of the pantry with the apple peeler he bought that devoured her apples.

Maggie was not entirely suspicious. She was guarded, observing strangers or new acquaintances from a distance. Jack was the one you brought your friends home to meet. He'd greet them like a holiday cruise captain. My girlfriends, and later my boyfriends, loved my Mark Twain story-telling father. They quickly sensed it was hard to impress my mother

"He's a good looker and a dapper dresser," was Jack's assessment of one heartthrob I brought home when I was dating.

Kneading bread dough in the pantry, Maggie heard

and shouted, "That handsome face might sprout warts later on, and if you ask me, a dapper dresser is often the sign of a selfish fellow."

In the flick of a few words, she could set you thinking.

"Beware of the good dancer," she warned, "He's not apt to be content beyond the ballroom. Hard to keep that kind at home. When the babies come along, he'll still want to be the center of attention."

When I asked her why she never praised us, she said, "All mothers think their children are swell but the world decides who really is. Better for you to be pleased later on than be let down by false expectations."

"Sometimes God gives the most important job to the most lowly. Look at His son Jesus," she said. "So poor, He was born in a barn."

When a friend who repeatedly borrowed money asked me for a loan, Maggie said I was a fool to lend it to her. The friend had overlooked paying me back in the past. Like my father, I'd never mention the outstanding debt for fear of losing a friend. In defense of my judgment, I told my mother that this friend would give me the shirt off her back if I needed it.

"Oh yeah," she said with hand on hip, "Did you ever notice that you're always the one with the shirt to lend? Where, may I ask, is she hiding hers?"

"Say no," she advised, "it only hurts a true friend for a minute".

So, my friend's fifty-eight-year-old mother did not take driving lessons at my expense, but at someone else's. Secretly, I felt my refusal justified, when my friend's mother didn't pass the road test.

In my youth, I thought her ridiculous because she claimed to prefer living in the less affluent neighborhoods. Her contention was that people with money can take care of their own, and they expect you to do the same. The lower the rent, the kinder, the more thoughtful the neighbors. "Self sufficiency isn't always a bonus," she said. Every time I hear Barbra Striesand sing, "People who need people" I think of my mother's words.

When we moved from a city flat to the single family country house my father bought as a surprise for her, my mother's sisters envied her. My mother was miserable. She missed access to public transportation and the friendly women she met over the back porch clothesline or ones she chatted with on the front stoop afternoons.

It was no surprise that within five years, we found ourselves back in the city living in a bank owned Somerville flat. My father had lost his job as a traffic manager and the house as well. My mother explained, "It was God's will." Her children knew it was hers as well. The truth was we had to move to the city where rents were lower.

In the sixties, when my husband and I told her we bought our first home in the suburbs of Boston, Maggie shook her finger at us: "Don't forget, once a month comes around fast." She meant our rent was too high. Her list of survival strategies was endless.

Observe people before you befriend, she warned, and it's wiser to be friendly with someone two doors down than right next door. Borrow if you must, but never return an empty bowl if you want to keep friends.

Maggie never read Confucius, Shakespeare or any of the sages in literature, yet when I first read them, I thought they had stolen her lines. With a lilt of an Irish brogue, she gave me advice similar to what Polonuis gave his son in Hamlet.

Our family was hardly material for a Waltons' TV script. The Ma-likes-you-better-than-me syndrome was prevalent. We were sarcastic to each other — sentimental behavior was scorned — we bonded only when the chips were down. A psychiatrist once told me sarcasm and disapproval was a cover-up for sexual feelings among siblings. It makes it easier for siblings to separate later in life when they must.

My mother was overwhelmed with the responsibility of keeping us fed and clothed let alone housekeeping. The latter, she did just barely. Laundry alone took two days. Her escape was the Catholic Church, and the close relationship she had with my Aunt Nora. Their big outing was a trip to Boston where they would scout Filene's Basement for bargains and attend Mass at the Franciscan Chapel on Arch Street. At home, she ruled like an unarmed five-star general. She picked up a broom when she got mad, though I rarely remember her making contact. Though she never used physical abuse, she yelled plenty, and deserved an award as a referee.

One morning the coffee percolator sailed through the air when Margaret threw it at Harry because he teased her so. Hot coffee splattered all over the kitchen. I was on Margaret's side that morning.

Another morning, I took too long at the kitchen mirror where we combed our hair, and Harry gave me a Three-Stooges head-banger. It hurt. I cried. My mother turned and gave him one.

"You're a big bully with your sisters, aren't you?" my mother shouted, hands on hips facing Harry. "If you did that to John, he'd flatten you. You ought to hang your head in shame."

My parents seldom fought loudly as their children did; they bickered. They only fought after one of my father's drinking sprees — and though everyone said my father became aggressive when he drank, we children never saw him that way. My mother would not allow him to come home. When he sobered up, sometimes a few days later, sometimes a week, we knew he acquired her forgiveness or had taken the pledge. It might be a year before it happened again, but it did, and then we would see him cower like the rest of us did when we did something wrong.

Maggie wore the proverbial black hat; Jack the white one. Though she seldom showed him affection in our presence, we knew she loved him. Children aren't always asleep when parents think they are. In sobriety, he had her respect. When it came to politics or world affairs, he read voraciously. When a leak, a chair, or a child's heart needed fixing, she turned to her Jack. His humor was their survival kit.

Maggie didn't display her love. Jack would encircle you with his brawny, freckled, hard-working arms. He'd cry if he hadn't seen you in a long time. Emotionally, I'm like my father. I will be forever grateful for his affectionate demonstrations. Maggie loved undemonstratively. After he died, she seemed surprised that her children willingly took good care of her. Every weekend one of us would pick her up so she wouldn't be alone. I think she thought we loved him best because we showed him affection. But he invited us to embrace or kiss him.

I envy people who have ideal families like the Waltons. It must be nice, but I feel we learned so much from each other. The lack of money during most of my growing years didn't bother me, but my father's drinking did.

One Christmas Eve, I think I was ten, he blew his paycheck, and my mother had to borrow money from my Aunt Kitty to put up a tree.

Another time, I think I was twenty, and was working in Washington, D.C., when my brother Patrick telephoned me.

"She kicked Pa out for good," he said.

"He must have been drinking," I said. "He knows she won't tolerate that nonsense."

Still in high school and living at home, Patrick was in the middle of it. I knew what he wanted from me.

So I telephoned my Dad from DC, told him that I too hated his drinking, that my biggest fear was that he would show up at my wedding drunk. He started to cry and then so did I.

"I missed you when you left," he said. "Your mother goes everywhere with Aunt Nora. The house was empty. I have no one to tell my jokes to."

When I was home, we often went to the movies or the racetrack together. Patrick was too busy socially. My other brothers were still in the service.

"Will you stop drinking if I come home?" He promised he would. The wartime job I was doing was ending anyhow. I left Washington about eight weeks later.

"She'll take you back if you promise to stay sober," I said. "I know she will." She did and he stayed sober for fifteen years and he was sober at my wedding. Then his doctor told him his heart was bad. I suspect he became fearful. They owned a grocery store and he couldn't avoid lifting tonic cases and such. He started to sip on the quiet, and because he didn't eat much, whatever he drank went right to his liver. He died at age 72 in 1959 and left a big void in all our lives. Thank God, I had two young children at the time or I would have fallen apart.

Somehow, I could always find excuses for my Dad, and deep inside I believed my strong mother made him weak. It took me years to understand their relationship. It wasn't her fault. We choose our spouses emotionally. I believe, we seek in our spouse what we feel we lack.

When I had left home at nineteen to work in Washington, he did not want me to leave. I overheard their conversation.

"Wartime Washington," he said, "is a dangerous place for a young girl."

"If we've done our job, she'll be all right. She'll go to Mass on Sunday and keep the commandments. I feel certain she will."

The war was a good excuse to use to lose your sense of self, but I was Maggie's daughter, and I made sure she was right about me, I never let her down.

She didn't cry when I left; she didn't cry when I returned. I came home for good after the war ended. On the front porch, I ran into our landlady who lived on the first floor. She hugged me and said she was glad I was home because my mother had cried her heart out at her kitchen table for weeks after I left home for Washington.

I climbed the stairs to that lovely flat in Everett we rented during the war. It had fireplaces in all the rooms, including the bedrooms. My mother sat at our new enameled topped kitchen table reading a newspaper. We dressed for travel in 1946. I wore a red, white, and blue tattersall capped-sleeved dress and a wide-brimmed navy-blue straw hat. I thought I looked just like the movie star, Rosalind Russell. I placed my luggage on the hall floor. "I'm home," I said gleefully as I stood at the kitchen door, my arms opened with hope. She looked up from her newspaper for one second and said,

"I like your hat."

The Family Secret

"Did you know your sister Margaret got married?" my mother asked me one morning as I poured coffee from the electric percolator. Fully dressed ready to leave for my job at the Telephone Company, I put the pot down and spun around.

"You're joking." I could tell by her expression she wasn't. "When did this happen?"

"A week or two ago. You didn't know? I thought surely she'd at least call you." Before this, guilt had prompted me to tell my mother I had clandestine meetings with the sister who was estranged from our family.

"Of course I want you to go see her if she calls you. She has no one," my mother had said months before when I told her I had met Margaret after work for dinner. But now, I could tell, my mother didn't know whether to believe me.

"How do you know?" I said, pouring Pets evaporated milk from a can into my coffee. It was years before I could drink coffee with ordinary milk.

"Aunt Kitty saw the announcement in the Boston Globe." Aunt Kitty was my mother's youngest sister.

"Can you beat that?" I said, "I haven't seen her for about six or eight months. She never mentioned she was dating anyone. I'm surprised she didn't call me. Whoever thought Margaret would marry?"

"She's so cold and distant, I wonder, how it will work. Never to call a soul. I don't understand my own child."

On my way to my friend Frannie's house the following Saturday afternoon, I cut across Perkins Street and stopped by my Aunt Kitty's house which was in proximity to hers. I decided to see for myself.

"Well what brings my niece to this part of the woods?" My Aunt's sarcasm was based on my neglect of her daughter. Aunt Kitty had only one child, a daughter she adored so she never cared about me like my Aunt Nora did. My cousin Katie was okay, but I needed friends who had less than me — not ones who had everything. Growing up, she was precocious, talked like a little old lady, and she let me know I was less fortunate. I envied her with her own room, fancy clothes, and piles of toys. I had felt drab beside her. In maturity, I had more friends, and was more independent. She paid dearly for my Aunt's devotion to her.

Now my Aunt Kitty showed me the marriage announcements in the Globe.

"I can't find it." I said.

"It's right there." My aunt pointed to a column I had

read over and over. "See, she's used her real father's name, Kelly.

"Who's Kelly? My father is her father."

"My God, Rosie, don't you know. I am talking about your mother's first husband, Tim Kelly." She says, pointing to the printed announcement. "See. Margaret took your father's name when he adopted her."

"You mean Margaret's adopted?" I glanced up from the page.

I sat down now. My mind was scrambling.

"No. Margaret's not adopted." A tone of impatience had crept into her voice.

My aunt tells my cousin to pour us a cup of tea. The kettle always simmers on a Nolan stove. Even in Ireland, they tell me.

"Rosie, both your mother and father have been married before. Your mother had two children: Margaret and Harry." She used her fingers to count. "Your father had three children, Marguerite, John and Arthur. After they married, they had Frank, Vincent, Rose and Patrick.

"I thought you knew," Aunt Kitty said. "I don't understand why she didn't tell you." My aunt shoveled three teaspoons of sugar into her tea. What luxury. I was brought up to use one and to stir twenty times so the sweetener went further. I felt strange. I looked around the room trying to focus elsewhere. It's a dream, I thought. But I couldn't dismiss what my aunt had told me.

I sat sipping my tea. My family was a deck of cards; I had to sort them, put my siblings in piles. Who went with my mother? With my father? It didn't seem right. Once, when a school chum asked me why I had a sister Margaret and a sister Marguerite, I went home and asked my mother.

"Because they're both named after me and I like my name," she said in her that's-that tone.

"What happened to her first husband?" I finally managed to speak to my aunt.

"Your mother was the envy of us all. The three of us, Nora, Maggie and myself worked together at Hood Rubber. Tim Kelly was a white collar worker, checked our time cards. Nora and I didn't dare talk to him, but Maggie ribbed him because he was a greenhorn not long off the boat from Ireland. Huh, as if we were Yankees.

"He was a serious young man. At first, he didn't know she was ribbing him, but then he ate lunch with us every day. We could tell he sat with us to be near her. Well, turns out he graduated from the University of Dublin — came here to teach school, but took the test a coupla times and couldn't get a certificate.

"A year or so afta they met, they were married. Tim turned out to be a high strung, serious man, bitter about the fact he couldn't teach in the states. Crankier than my Joe, if you can believe that — not a bit like your father. Thought he was better than the rest of us. Maggie wanted him to take a job on the line with us so he could make more money. He wouldn't, he was too proud. They were poor as church mice."

"So she divorced him."

"God no. No Nolan ever divorces. He died, five years after they married. From tuberculosis. Your sister Margaret was three, and Harry wasn't even born. I bet he had it when he came over. He always looked underfed. By some miracle no one else caught the bloody TB."

"Did he leave her any money?"

"Nary a farthing." This was an expression my mother often used to mean not a penny.

"Poor Maggie, she was pregnant and had to come home to live with us until Harry was born. Pa accused her of having her children illegitimately because she married Tim Kelly without his permission. She got married in your Aunt Mary's parish in Roxbury. She didn't tell Pa cause she didn't want him around — drunk that he was."

"How about Grandma? Was she good to her."

"Oh God yes, she was good to everyone, but she was terrified of his nibs. We all were. He could be brutal if brother Pat wasn't around. And oh boy, he had it in for poor Maggie. Had her in tears, calling her a whore and a tramp in front of us all. He called the young ones bastards. She cried herself to sleep many a night. No money and she'd just lost the man she thought was the cat's meow, mind ya."

"Why didn't she apply for welfare?"

"Sure you forget. There was no such thing before Roosevelt."

"Soon as she could, Maggie looked for a job as a domestic where she could bring her kids along with her. By the time baby Harry was six months old, she had answered eighty-four newspaper ads in handwriting. When she got a response, Ma would mind the kids while she went on interviews if the old man wasn't around. But it was hard; he cobbled shoes at home. Maggie dragged those tots, one on the hip and one on the hand, on the streetcar. That's if your Uncle Pat or myself gave her the money for carfare.

"She'd come home and tell me all about the job interviews because your aunts, Nora and Mary, were married by then. Things were pretty rough. No one had money. One day she came home all excited. A widower in Brookline she went to see seemed interested. He had a lovely house that overlooked the reservoir. A banker, she thought. His wife died leaving him with two children under ten. The house was a mansion, Maggie said.

"But that very day a letter from your father was waiting for her. She let me read it. 'Dear Margaret Josephine,' he wrote. He had fine handwriting your father. He sounded desperate. His wife had died from diabetes. He had one girl and two boys, who needed someone with "a good heart," as he put it. His housekeeper had taken his food home to her own, leaving his kids hungry, and she was too quick to smack them for no reason. He wouldn't mind at all if the applicant brought along her children as long as she would treat them all alike. He needed someone right away and was willing to drive to Cambridge from South Boston to get her and the children for an interview

"Poor man,' your mother said.

"She walked to the drugstore and phoned him. The next day, he came in his car to get her with her kiddos.

'That night she told me, she was going to work for your father. 'What about the banker?' I asked.

'He needs me more than the banker. He's a good man, doesn't drink and he has holy pictures all over his wall. I know I can trust him. And he likes kids. Right away, he took baby Harry in his arm and cooed to him. His poor kids look neglected. The housekeeper stole all the sheets off the kids' beds. The little girl acts like a mother wiping her brothers' nose and all,' Maggie said. 'She's in an apron cleaning up the place when I got there. Oh, and he said, I could have Saturday afternoon and all day Sunday to myself. He's not rich, but he's got a pretty good job.'

"I would have gone with the banker," my aunt said.

Even after my aunt told me all this, I couldn't understand why my mother hadn't told me herself. If she had been divorced, I could understand. Catholics then felt shame about divorce. Why did my parents feel they had something to hide? Had I lied when I bragged to the nuns and priest that I came from a family of nine? The celibate nuns always blessed my mother for "Bringing all those souls to God."

"When did my parents marry?" I focused long enough to ask.

"About two years later. Instead of coming home for Sunday dinners, gradually, she stayed at Jack's. Sometimes Jack would come and pick me and Mum up for Sunday dinner at his house. He was a wonderful cook. We all took to him. Liked him much better than skin-and-brains Kelly."

My aunt felt bad for me. As I left her house that day, she stood at her door and said,

"For God's sakes Rosie, don't tell her I told you. I don't fit as it is." Kitty was right. The Nolan sisters felt Kitty flaunted her superior economic status. She didn't. It was just that her husband worked steady, and she had only one child to care for. My sister Marguerite told me Aunt Kitty told her how she felt about her sisters' frequent pregnancies. "Too bad they let those Italian Bozos in Rome tell them what to do."

After I left Kitty's, I was so upset I never got to my friend Frannie's house. Instead, I rushed home intending to confront my mother. I marched in the back door, looked at my mother who now sat at the kitchen window staring out and saying her daily Novenas to Blessed Martin, St. Joseph and St. Francis of Assisi, and my anger turned to sympathy. Besides, I couldn't figure out how to tell her what I knew without implicating Aunt Kitty.

I never mustered courage to confront my mother. After what Aunt Kitty told me about my mother's first marriage, I figured she had endured enough hurt in her life. My mother had created a shield to cover feelings too hard to share. If we asked, she gave us her generation's refrains. "You have no idea what poverty is," or "what you don't know won't hurt you." She had told us her father was an abusive drunk but never gave us details.

It bothered me that my cousin Kate knew and I had been left out of the loop. I dwelt on it for a while, then I forgot about it. For nineteen years, I had never thought of my siblings as my mother's children or my father's children, or as half brothers and sisters, but as my full-blooded siblings. At least, I was related to everyone. I never changed my original mindset. Maybe I was angry I wasn't told, but I think I was more curious about the needless deception.

♣ ♣ ♣

It wasn't until years later; in fact, I was 38, when my mother revealed the same family secret.

My husband had secretly asked my mother to visit us that weekend. Five months into a pregnancy, a child had died in my womb and I cried frequently. My tearful outbursts seemed endless to him though it had only been eight weeks since the misfortune.

My mother and I sat on our living room couch after dinner. George had gone back to work at a motel he was managing. She fingered and praised the brown denim slipcover with yellow piping I had made. Both children were asleep. By now, we had a son, seven, and a daughter five. They were born after two painful and unsuccessful pregnancies. A tubal pregnancy that ended at three months, and another child I carried eight and a half months that had lived only seven hours. The most recent child died in my womb at five months.

Not only that, my husband had just lost a business he had started with all our savings. The mortgagee of the building he rented foreclosed on his restaurant for non-payment of rent. The business had failed after two years. The Internal Revenue Service haunted us for back taxes. We had owned our suburban house for two years, and now we were on the brink of losing it. I felt like a failure. I would look at my children and cry. thinking how I wanted them so much, and now we couldn't support them properly. My mother sat beside me crocheting one of her tri-colored zigzag afghans. This one may have been started for my baby.

"What would you like to watch on TV?"

"Nothing special," she said. When I got up to turn it on, she started to talk. Until then, my loss was like the proverbial elephant in the middle of the room.

"I know how you must feel, losing the baby an all," she said. "I was in terrible shape after I lost Baby Vincent. I spun into a deep depression, wouldn't eat and cried all the time. Dr. Davey thought I was having a nervous breakdown. Jack took me to Boston City where psychiatrists questioned me for hours.

"That's right, baby Vincent." I stopped changing channels and turned to look at her. "You always said he was an angel in heaven because he was baptized."

Now I walked toward her. "That's what the priest told me when I lost my first infant. A Catholic nurse had given our infant son conditional baptism. Frankly, Mom, it didn't make me feel any better. I wanted to scream at him 'I don't want an angel in heaven, I want a baby in my arms'."

Whenever I had a conflict with the Church or its authority, I blamed my mother. It was her fault they harassed me about marrying a non-Catholic. Her fault they almost killed me with their rhythm method. Her fault I could never turn my back on the Church. My grievances were the same as those of many women of my day. But now, I was beginning to envy her implicit faith. What would she have done without it? I was at a time in my life, when I wished I had more. I sat beside her on the couch again.

"Did the psychiatrists help you?"

"I had plenty to tell them, but it turned out it wasn't my lousy childhood, or even my depression that made me sick. After weeks of blah, blah, blah, they found I had a large abscess on the brain. In those days, rest was the only cure for infection. They put me in a sanatorium for six months. Poor Jack was left with all our kids to care for. Aunt Nora, God love her, lived nearby and she was a big help to him. I almost lost the will to live. But I prayed daily to the Virgin Mary. She got me home to my children three months earlier than expected. That all happened before you were born."

Her seventy-five-year-old blue-veined hand worked

the bone needle feverishly, she held a stitch, then looked up at me and grinned.

"Course not long after I got home, I got pregnant. The doctor had a fit. Course he wasn't Catholic." She laughed aloud at this. "That's when you were born. Your birth was a blessing. Lifted me out of the doldrums. I wanted to name you Mary, but your father wouldn't hear of it. That was his awful stepmother's name. So I named you Rose because you were born in the month of June, the month of roses. Not only that, but Our Lady loved roses. Did you know that?"

"Yes, Mom, I did. You told me years ago. It was once when I brought you home a bouquet of roses from the greenhouses in Revere. I remember you told me that when I asked why you put my flowers in front of the Blessed Virgin statue on your bedroom bureau."

If greenhouse employees cut the discarded roses too short for market they tossed them into a pile at their backdoor. They were usually perfect flowers. Children picked the pile two or three times a day.

"Seems like yesterday sometimes, other times it seems like centuries ago," she said, wistfully. We were silent for a while. Perhaps we were each focusing on the past. I spoke first.

"Good Lord, Mum, you really did have a tough life."

"Others had it worse." she responded quickly almost defensively. "Your Grandmother for instance. At least I had two kind husbands."

Then, she told me the same story my Aunt Kitty

had told me when I was nineteen. She talked about how cruel my Grandfather was to her after her first husband Tim died; about why she chose my father. She laughed when she talked about my father. He had been dead four years by then.

"He was not only good looking, he was the picture of sanctity. You couldn't see the walls for the holy pictures: St. Anthony, Our Lady of Perpetual Help. I found out later they belonged to his dead wife." She waved to pictures on my walls to illustrate. "Then, the rascal had the unmitigated gall to tell me he never drank." She smiled at first, then looked away her eyes filled with longing for him.

"And he didn't. Not while he was caring for those motherless children. He knew he couldn't stop at one drink. No man loved his children the way Jack did. You, of all people, know that. I knew he couldn't help himself. That's why I always took him back."

"Why didn't you ever tell us this stuff before? I think it would have helped us all to understand so much." I don't know why, but I still didn't tell her I knew. Maybe I didn't want to spoil the moment, the intimacy, or maybe I still wanted to keep my promise to my now deceased Aunt Kitty.

I thought of my half-brothers and sisters, losing a parent so young, and never allowed mourning the loss aloud. My sister Margaret not only lost her father; she lost her mother to another family of children when she needed her the most. No wonder she sabotaged relationships. Keeping the secret had to affect each of my parent's children. How difficult it must have been for my mother and my father to try to fill another parent's shoes. No wonder my mother blamed herself for John's running away.

"I'd have understood so much if only I had known growing up," I said. I wanted to hug my mother. Cry on her shoulder, tell her how sorry I was for all her loss and pain. But since she made no overture, I didn't dare. Old habits die hard. After I married, I would kiss her on the cheek when I hadn't seen her for a while. She never kissed or hugged me. The only time I embraced her was when she was dying of cancer in her hospital bed in 1965, she was pleased but uncomfortable even then. What I remember most about her last days was her deep gratitude for whatever we did for her. Despite her pain, she expressed her appreciation constantly.

"Why didn't you tell me all this before?" I said, returning to our conversation.

"Jack and I decided it would be too confusing for kids in one family with two names. Too many questions asked. The older kids knew. We told them not to tell you younger ones. What you didn't know wouldn't hurt you. We didn't blab our business on every street corner like you kids do today. We took our lumps and kept our mouth shut. Offering hardship up for the souls in purgatory." Then she stopped her needle, took a breath to regain the composure she was beginning to lose to tears. She adjusted her bifocals so she could see me correctly, looked into my eyes and said,

"Besides, I hate it when people feel sorry for me. Don't you?"

About the Author

Photo by Dorothy Stone

Rose Gotsis, poet and writer, is the last living member of a large Irish-American Catholic family of nine children (one child died as an infant). She shares her life with the reader to demonstrate how well children of working class immigrant parents functioned despite the Depression and World War II. She is proud to be a member of the generation who created the superior, pluralistic society Americans now enjoy. Irish Stew illustrates how faith, humor and grace help us all to survive hard times. Raised in a narrow Boston-Irish culture, her relatives were surprised when in 1951 she married a first-generation Greek. Since her husband was a Hotel Manager, they moved frequently until 1961 when they settled in west suburban Boston where they still live. They have two children, three adult grandchildren and a new great-grandchild. The author's poetry and prose have earned several awards and have appeared in literary magazines, newspapers and national publications. Her OP-Ed pieces and Book Reviews have been published in the Metro West Daily News since 1991. She is a Senior Editor of the Longfellow Society Journal. This is her first book of prose.